WE ARE GODS

Dr. Maxwell Shimba

Shimba Publishing, LLC.

Printed in the United States of America

SHIMBA
PUBLISHING

TABLE OF CONTENTS

INTRODUCTION

We Are Gods on Earth

Embracing Our Divine Identity

John 10:34: "Jesus answered them, 'Is it not written in your Law, "I have said you are 'gods'"?'"

The notion that we are gods on earth is a profound and often misunderstood concept. Rooted in biblical scripture and affirmed by the teachings of Jesus Christ, this idea challenges us to explore the depths of our identity and our divine calling. This chapter serves as an introduction to understanding what it means to be gods on earth, drawing from both the Old and New Testaments, and setting the stage for a deeper exploration of our spiritual heritage and responsibilities.

The Biblical Foundation

The foundation of this concept is found in the scriptures, particularly in Psalm 82:6 and John 10:34. These passages provide the theological basis for understanding our divine nature and calling.

1. Psalm 82:6: "I said, 'You are "gods"; you are all sons of the Most High.'" In this psalm, God addresses the judges of Israel, calling them "gods" because of their role in administering His justice and representing His authority on

earth. This title signifies their divine appointment and the weight of their responsibilities (Psalm 82:6-7).

2. John 10:34: Jesus reaffirms this concept when He responds to the Pharisees' accusations of blasphemy. By quoting Psalm 82:6, Jesus emphasizes that those who receive God's Word are given divine status and authority. This serves as a reminder of our potential to reflect God's character and exercise His authority in our lives (John 10:34-36).

Understanding Our Divine Identity

Understanding that we are gods on earth requires a deep exploration of our creation, purpose, and relationship with God. This identity is not about self-exaltation but about recognizing our divine origin and living out our God-given purpose.

1. Created in God's Image: From the beginning, humanity was created in the image and likeness of God (Genesis 1:26-27). This divine imprint gives us inherent worth and the capacity to reflect God's nature. It calls us to live in a way that honors our Creator and fulfills His purposes for our lives.

2. Divine Appointment: Just as the judges in Psalm 82 were appointed to carry out God's justice, we too are appointed to represent God's kingdom on earth. This appointment comes with the responsibility to live righteously,

promote justice, and extend God's love and grace to others (2 Corinthians 5:20).

3. Union with Christ: Through faith in Jesus Christ, we are united with Him and become partakers in His divine nature (2 Peter 1:4). This union empowers us to live out our divine calling and to walk in the authority and power that come from our relationship with Him.

The Responsibilities of Being Gods on Earth

Embracing our identity as gods on earth comes with significant responsibilities. We are called to reflect God's character, exercise His authority, and fulfill His purposes in our daily lives.

1. Reflecting God's Character: As gods on earth, we are called to reflect God's holiness, love, and righteousness. This involves living in a way that honors Him and demonstrates His attributes to the world. Our actions, words, and attitudes should mirror the character of our Creator (Ephesians 5:1-2).

2. Exercising Divine Authority: God has entrusted us with authority to carry out His will on earth. This authority is exercised through prayer, proclamation of the gospel, and acts of justice and mercy. We are called to stand against evil, promote good, and advance God's kingdom in our spheres of influence (Luke 10:19).

3. Fulfilling God's Purposes: Our divine identity comes with a mission to fulfill God's purposes. This involves using our gifts, talents, and resources to serve others and to make a positive impact on the world. We are called to be agents of change, bringing hope, healing, and transformation to those around us (Matthew 28:18-20).

The Challenges of Living as Gods on Earth

While our divine identity is a source of great privilege and responsibility, it also comes with challenges. Recognizing and overcoming these challenges is essential for living out our calling effectively.

1. Overcoming Self-Centeredness: One of the greatest challenges is overcoming the temptation to use our divine status for self-centered purposes. True divinity is marked by humility and a commitment to serve others rather than seeking personal glory (Philippians 2:3-8).

2. Resisting Temptation: As gods on earth, we face spiritual warfare and the constant temptation to stray from God's path. We must remain vigilant, grounded in God's Word, and reliant on the Holy Spirit to resist temptation and live faithfully (Ephesians 6:10-18).

3. Enduring Persecution: Living as gods on earth often means standing against the values and norms of the world, which can lead to persecution and opposition. We are called

to endure these challenges with grace, knowing that our ultimate reward comes from God (2 Timothy 3:12).

The Impact of Embracing Our Divine Identity

When we fully embrace our identity as gods on earth, it transforms not only our lives but also the world around us. This transformation is marked by a greater sense of purpose, empowerment, and influence.

1. Greater Purpose: Understanding our divine identity gives our lives greater meaning and direction. We live with a sense of purpose that transcends earthly pursuits and is rooted in God's eternal plans (Jeremiah 29:11).

2. Empowerment: Embracing our divine identity empowers us to live boldly and confidently. We are equipped with the Holy Spirit's power to overcome challenges, perform miracles, and fulfill God's purposes (Acts 1:8).

3. Influence: Our lives become a testimony of God's power and grace, influencing others to seek and know Him. As we reflect God's character and exercise His authority, we draw people to the transformative love of Christ (Matthew 5:14-16).

Conclusion: Embracing the Journey

As we embark on this journey to understand and live out our identity as gods on earth, we must continually seek God's guidance and strength. This introductory chapter sets the foundation for exploring the depths of our divine calling and responsibilities. Through the following chapters, we will delve deeper into the practical and spiritual aspects of living as gods on earth, empowered by God's Spirit and grounded in His Word.

May we embrace this divine identity with humility, courage, and a commitment to fulfill God's purposes in our lives and in the world. Let us walk in the truth of who we are, reflecting God's glory and advancing His kingdom on earth.

DR. MAXWELL SHIMBA

CHAPTER 01

KNOWING GOD

Understanding the nature and character of God is foundational to the Christian faith. It is through this understanding that believers can deepen their relationship with Him, experiencing His love, grace, and power in transformative ways. This chapter explores various attributes of God, revealing who He is and how these attributes impact our lives.

The Incomprehensibility of God

God's nature is vast and beyond full human comprehension. This incomprehensibility is not a barrier to knowing God but rather an invitation to a lifelong journey of discovery and relationship.

1. Infinite and Eternal: God is infinite, having no limitations in space or time, and eternal, existing without beginning or end. This attribute assures us of His constant presence and unchanging nature (Psalm 90:2).

2. Transcendent and Immanent: God transcends His creation, existing beyond and independent from it, yet He is also immanent, meaning He is present and active within His creation. This duality means that while God is far greater than we can imagine, He is also intimately involved in our lives (Isaiah 57:15).

3. Mystery and Revelation: While God's ways and thoughts are higher than ours, He has chosen to reveal Himself to us through creation, scripture, and ultimately through Jesus Christ. This revelation allows us to know Him personally and to understand His will for our lives (Romans 11:33, John 1:18).

The Holiness of God

God's holiness is a central attribute that defines His nature. It encompasses His absolute purity, moral perfection, and separation from all sin.

1. Absolute Purity: God is completely pure and without any trace of sin or evil. His holiness sets the standard for moral excellence and calls us to live in purity and righteousness (1 Peter 1:15-16).

2. Moral Perfection: God's actions and judgments are always just and right. His holiness ensures that He cannot tolerate sin and must respond to it with perfect justice. This

attribute assures us that we can trust God to be fair and righteous in all His ways (Deuteronomy 32:4).

3. Call to Holiness: As God is holy, He calls His people to be holy. This call to holiness involves being set apart for God's purposes, living in obedience to His commands, and reflecting His character in our lives (Leviticus 19:2).

The Love of God

God's love is perhaps the most celebrated of His attributes. It is through His love that He reaches out to humanity, offering salvation and a relationship with Him.

1. Unconditional Love: God's love is unconditional, meaning it is not based on our actions or worthiness. He loves us because of who He is, not because of who we are. This love is demonstrated most clearly through the sacrifice of Jesus Christ (Romans 5:8).

2. Sacrificial Love: God's love is sacrificial, giving of Himself for our sake. The greatest expression of this love is seen in Jesus' willingness to die on the cross for our sins, providing a way for us to be reconciled with God (John 3:16).

3. Transformative Love: God's love has the power to transform our lives. It heals our brokenness, gives us new purpose, and empowers us to love others. Experiencing God's love compels us to share it with the world (1 John 4:19).

The Sovereignty of God

God's sovereignty means that He is the supreme ruler over all creation. He has ultimate authority and power, and His plans and purposes cannot be thwarted.

1. Ultimate Authority: God's sovereignty assures us that He has control over all things. He governs the universe with wisdom and power, and nothing happens outside of His will. This gives us confidence in His ability to guide our lives and bring about His purposes (Isaiah 46:9-10).

2. Providence: God's sovereignty is exercised through His providence, whereby He sustains and directs all things. He works in and through circumstances to accomplish His divine plans, often in ways that we may not understand but can trust completely (Romans 8:28).

3. Response to Sovereignty: Understanding God's sovereignty leads us to a posture of trust and surrender. We can rest in the knowledge that God is in control, even in difficult times, and we can confidently follow His leading, knowing that His plans are for our good (Jeremiah 29:11).

The Omnipotence of God

God's omnipotence refers to His all-powerful nature. He is able to do anything that is consistent with His character and will.

1. Unlimited Power: There is nothing that God cannot do. His power is infinite and encompasses all things in heaven

and on earth. This attribute reassures us of His ability to fulfill His promises and intervene in our lives (Jeremiah 32:17).

2. Miracles and Creation: God's omnipotence is displayed in the creation of the universe and the miracles recorded in Scripture. From speaking the world into existence to raising the dead, God's mighty works reveal His power and glory (Genesis 1:1, Luke 1:37).

3. Empowering Believers: God's omnipotence is also at work within believers, empowering us to live out our faith and accomplish His purposes. Through the Holy Spirit, we are given the strength and ability to do what we could not do on our own (Ephesians 3:20).

The Omniscience of God

God's omniscience means that He knows everything—past, present, and future. His knowledge is complete and perfect.

1. Complete Knowledge: God's knowledge is exhaustive. He knows every detail of creation, every thought and intention of the heart, and every future event. This attribute assures us that nothing is hidden from God and that He understands us fully (Psalm 139:1-4).

2. Wisdom and Guidance: God's omniscience is coupled with His wisdom, which He uses to guide and direct

our lives. He knows what is best for us and leads us according to His perfect knowledge and plan (Proverbs 3:5-6).

3. Comfort in God's Knowledge: Knowing that God understands everything about our lives brings comfort and security. We can trust Him with our concerns, knowing that He is aware of our needs and is working for our good (Matthew 6:8).

The Faithfulness of God

God's faithfulness means that He is reliable and trustworthy. He keeps His promises and is steadfast in His love and commitment to His people.

1. Promise Keeper: God is always faithful to His promises. What He has said, He will do. This attribute gives us confidence in His Word and assurance that He will fulfill His covenant with us (Numbers 23:19).

2. Steadfast Love: God's faithfulness is a reflection of His steadfast love. He remains committed to us even when we falter, continually offering His grace and mercy. This love encourages us to remain faithful to Him in return (Lamentations 3:22-23).

3. Faithfulness in Trials: In times of trial and difficulty, God's faithfulness is our anchor. We can rely on His unchanging nature and trust that He is with us, providing

strength and hope through every circumstance (1 Corinthians 10:13).

Knowing God is the greatest pursuit of our lives. As we grow in our understanding of His nature and character, we are drawn into deeper relationship with Him. The attributes of God—His incomprehensibility, holiness, love, sovereignty, omnipotence, omniscience, and faithfulness—reveal a God who is worthy of our worship and trust. By embracing these truths, we are transformed and empowered to live lives that honor Him and reflect His glory. May we continue to seek to know God more fully, experiencing the richness of His presence and the depth of His love in every aspect of our lives.

HOLINESS OF GOD

"The Knowledge of the Holy" Let us focus on the holiness of God, a central and defining attribute that permeates every aspect of His being. Understanding God's holiness transforms our perception of Him and profoundly impacts our worship and daily lives.

The Essence of God's Holiness

The holiness of God is His intrinsic and transcendent purity, moral perfection, and separation from all that is profane. It is not merely one attribute among many, but the crown of His nature and the sum of all His attributes.

1. Intrinsic Purity: God's holiness is His inherent and unchanging purity. He is entirely free from sin, evil, and any form of moral corruption. This purity is absolute and infinite, setting Him apart from all creation (1 John 1:5).

2. Moral Perfection: Holiness encompasses God's perfect moral character. His actions, thoughts, and intentions are always just, righteous, and good. God's holiness is the standard of moral excellence and the foundation of His righteous judgments (Deuteronomy 32:4).

3. Transcendence and Immanence: God's holiness means He is transcendent, existing beyond and above the physical universe. Yet, He is also immanent, actively involved in His creation. His holiness sets Him apart while His presence draws near to redeem and sanctify (Isaiah 57:15).

The Revelation of God's Holiness

God reveals His holiness through His creation, His Word, and His Son, Jesus Christ. Each of these revelations provides a glimpse into the majesty and purity of the divine nature.

1. Creation's Testimony: The natural world reflects God's holiness. The order, beauty, and complexity of creation testify to the purity and perfection of the Creator. The heavens declare the glory of God, and the skies proclaim the work of His hands (Psalm 19:1).

2. Scriptural Revelation: The Bible is replete with declarations of God's holiness. From the call of Moses at the burning bush to the vision of Isaiah in the temple, Scripture reveals God's holy nature and His call for His people to be holy (Exodus 3:5, Isaiah 6:3).

3. Jesus Christ: The ultimate revelation of God's holiness is found in Jesus Christ. He embodies the holiness of God in human form, living a sinless life and providing the means for our sanctification through His death and resurrection. In Christ, we see the perfect expression of God's holy love and justice (Colossians 1:19-20).

The Impact of God's Holiness on Believers

Understanding God's holiness has a profound impact on believers. It shapes our worship, compels us to live holy lives, and transforms our relationship with God.

1. Reverent Worship: God's holiness evokes awe and reverence in worship. Recognizing His purity and majesty leads us to approach Him with humility and deep respect. True worship acknowledges God's holiness and responds with adoration and praise (Hebrews 12:28-29).

2. Call to Holiness: Believers are called to reflect God's holiness in their lives. This involves a commitment to moral purity, ethical living, and separation from sin. As God is holy, we are called to be holy in all that we do (1 Peter 1:15-16).

3. Transformative Relationship: God's holiness transforms our relationship with Him. It exposes our sinfulness and our need for repentance and sanctification. Through the Holy Spirit, we are continually being made holy, conforming to the image of Christ (2 Corinthians 3:18).

Holiness and the Fear of the Lord

The holiness of God instills a healthy fear of the Lord, which is essential for wisdom and spiritual growth. This fear is not terror but a profound respect and awe for God's majesty and righteousness.

1. Beginning of Wisdom: The fear of the Lord is the beginning of wisdom. It leads us to acknowledge God's authority and submit to His will. This reverence is foundational for understanding and living according to God's principles (Proverbs 9:10).

2. Moral Compass: A healthy fear of the Lord serves as a moral compass, guiding our decisions and actions. It reminds us of the seriousness of sin and the importance of living in a way that honors God. This fear motivates us to pursue righteousness and avoid evil (Proverbs 8:13).

3. Protection and Guidance: The fear of the Lord offers protection and guidance. It keeps us from straying into sin and aligns our hearts with God's purposes. Those who fear

the Lord find security and direction in His wisdom (Psalm 25:12-14).

The Holiness of God in the Life of Jesus

Jesus Christ, as the Son of God, perfectly embodies and reveals the holiness of God. His life, teachings, and sacrificial death demonstrate the holy love and justice of God.

1. Sinless Life: Jesus lived a sinless life, fully obedient to the Father's will. His purity and moral perfection are the ultimate expressions of God's holiness. In Him, we see what it means to live a holy life in complete alignment with God's purposes (Hebrews 4:15).

2. Teaching and Miracles: Jesus' teachings and miracles reveal the holy character of God. His words call people to repentance and holy living, while His miracles demonstrate God's power and compassion. Through Jesus, God's holiness is made manifest in the world (Matthew 5:48, John 14:10-11).

3. Sacrificial Death: The crucifixion of Jesus is the ultimate demonstration of God's holy love and justice. Through His sacrificial death, Jesus provides atonement for sin, satisfying the demands of God's holiness and offering redemption to humanity. His resurrection confirms His victory over sin and death, inviting us into a holy relationship with God (Romans 3:25-26, 1 Peter 2:24).

Living in the Light of God's Holiness

Believers are called to live in the light of God's holiness, allowing His holy nature to shape every aspect of their lives.

1. Personal Holiness: Personal holiness involves a commitment to purity, integrity, and ethical living. It requires regular self-examination, repentance, and reliance on the Holy Spirit to transform our hearts and minds. By striving for holiness, we honor God and reflect His character to the world (2 Corinthians 7:1).

2. Communal Holiness: Holiness is not only personal but also communal. The church, as the body of Christ, is called to be a holy community, marked by love, unity, and purity. Together, believers support and encourage one another in the pursuit of holiness, demonstrating God's holy nature to the world (Ephesians 4:1-3, 1 Peter 2:9).

3. Missional Holiness: Living in the light of God's holiness means engaging in His mission to the world. This involves proclaiming the gospel, serving others with compassion, and working for justice and righteousness. Our holy lives become a testimony of God's transformative power and a beacon of hope to those in darkness (Matthew 28:18-20, Micah 6:8).

The holiness of God is a profound and central attribute that defines His nature and shapes our relationship with Him. Understanding and revering God's holiness leads us to worship Him with awe, live lives of moral purity and integrity, and engage in His mission to the world. As we grow in our knowledge of God's holiness, we are transformed by His presence and empowered to reflect His holy nature in every aspect of our lives. May we continually seek to know the holy God more deeply, allowing His holiness to permeate our hearts and transform our lives for His glory.

CREATED IN HIS IMAGE

Genesis 1:27: "So God created mankind in his own image, in the image of God he created them; male and female he created them."

The Foundational Truth

The Bible begins with a powerful declaration: humans are made in the image of God. This foundational truth means that every person carries intrinsic worth and dignity. Our identity is not derived from our achievements, social status, or possessions but from the Creator Himself. To be made in God's image is to reflect His character, creativity, and authority in the world.

The Image of God in Us

To understand what it means to be created in God's image, we must first explore the nature of God Himself. God is spirit (John 4:24), eternal (Revelation 1:8), all-knowing (Psalm 147:5), and all-powerful (Jeremiah 32:17). He is holy, just, loving, and merciful. While we, as humans, do not possess these attributes to their fullest extent, we reflect aspects of God's nature in our being.

1. Spirituality: Humans are not just physical beings but also spiritual. We have the capacity for a relationship with God, the ability to worship, and the desire for meaning and purpose beyond the material world.

2. Eternality: Though our physical bodies are mortal, our souls are eternal. We are created with an eternal destiny, either in communion with God or separated from Him.

3. Intellect: God has endowed us with the ability to think, reason, and create. This intellectual capacity reflects God's omniscience and His role as the ultimate Creator.

4. Moral Agency: We have been given the ability to discern right from wrong and make moral choices. This reflects God's holiness and justice.

5. Relationality: Just as God exists in a perfect relationship within the Trinity (Father, Son, and Holy Spirit), humans are created for relationships with one another. Love, community, and fellowship are central to our existence.

The Dignity of Humanity

Understanding that we are made in God's image gives us a profound sense of dignity and worth. Every human being, regardless of their status, abilities, or background, is valuable in God's eyes. This truth has far-reaching implications for how we view ourselves and others.

1. Self-Worth: Our worth is intrinsic, not based on external factors. This frees us from the need to seek validation through achievements, possessions, or the approval of others. We are valuable simply because we are God's creation.

2. Respect for Others: Recognizing that every person is made in the image of God compels us to treat others with respect and dignity. This includes those who are different from us or whom society may deem less valuable. Each person is a reflection of the divine and deserves to be treated with honor and compassion.

3. Sanctity of Life: The belief in the inherent value of human life forms the basis for our convictions about the sanctity of life. This impacts our views on issues such as abortion, euthanasia, and the treatment of the marginalized and oppressed.

Reflecting God's Character

To be made in God's image is not just about inherent worth; it also carries a responsibility. We are called to reflect

God's character in the world. This means living in a way that mirrors His holiness, love, justice, and mercy.

1. Holiness: God calls us to live holy lives, set apart for His purposes (1 Peter 1:15-16). This involves striving for purity in our thoughts, words, and actions, and avoiding sin.

2. Love: Jesus summarized the law with two commands: love God and love your neighbor (Matthew 22:37-39). Reflecting God's image means loving others selflessly and sacrificially, just as He loves us.

3. Justice: God is a God of justice, and He calls us to act justly, love mercy, and walk humbly with Him (Micah 6:8). This involves standing up for the oppressed, defending the vulnerable, and working towards a fair and equitable society.

4. Mercy: Just as God is merciful, we are called to show mercy to others (Luke 6:36). This means forgiving those who wrong us, showing compassion to those in need, and extending grace to those who fall short.

The Creative Mandate

One aspect of being made in God's image is our ability to create. God, the ultimate Creator, has endowed us with creativity and the mandate to steward His creation.

1. Creativity: Our creativity reflects God's nature. Whether through art, music, literature, science, or technology, we express the creative aspect of our divine image.

2. Stewardship: In Genesis 1:28, God commands humanity to fill the earth and subdue it, exercising dominion over all living things. This mandate is not a license for exploitation but a call to stewardship. We are to care for the earth responsibly, ensuring that it flourishes for future generations.

The Distortion of the Image

While we are created in God's image, sin has marred that image. The fall of humanity brought about a distortion in our reflection of God's character. Our relationship with God was broken, and our ability to fully reflect His image was compromised.

1. Sin's Impact: Sin affects every aspect of our being—spiritual, intellectual, moral, and relational. It distorts our understanding of God, ourselves, and others. The result is brokenness in our lives and in the world.

2. Redemption in Christ: The good news is that through Jesus Christ, the image of God in us can be restored. Jesus is the perfect image of the invisible God (Colossians 1:15), and through His life, death, and resurrection, we are being renewed in His image (Colossians 3:10). This process of sanctification involves becoming more like Christ each day, as we surrender to the Holy Spirit's work in our lives.

Living Out Our Identity

Understanding that we are created in God's image calls us to live out that identity in practical ways. This involves embracing our worth, reflecting God's character, exercising our creativity, and participating in the work of redemption.

1. Embrace Your Worth: Recognize and affirm your value as a person made in God's image. Let this truth shape your self-perception and free you from seeking validation from external sources.

2. Reflect God's Character: Strive to live a life that mirrors God's holiness, love, justice, and mercy. Seek to grow in these areas through prayer, study of Scripture, and active discipleship.

3. Exercise Your Creativity: Use your creative gifts to honor God and bless others. Whether through artistic expression, problem-solving, or innovation, let your creativity reflect the Creator.

4. Participate in Redemption: Join God in His work of restoring and renewing the world. This can involve sharing the gospel, serving others, advocating for justice, and caring for creation.

In conclusion, being created in God's image is a profound truth that shapes every aspect of our lives. It gives us intrinsic worth, calls us to reflect God's character, empowers us to create, and invites us to participate in His redemptive work. As we embrace this identity and live it out, we fulfill the purpose for which we were created, bringing glory to God and blessing to the world.

CHAPTER 02

CHOSEN AND BELOVED

Ephesians 1:4-5: "For he chose us in him before the creation of the world to be holy and blameless in his sight. In love, he predestined us for adoption to sonship through Jesus Christ, in accordance with his pleasure and will."

God's love for us is not conditional. Before the world was formed, He chose us to be His own. This choice is rooted in His love and grace, not our merit. Understanding that we are chosen and beloved by God gives us a secure identity and purpose. It reminds us that our lives are part of a divine plan, orchestrated by a loving Father.

The Mystery of Divine Choice

The idea that God chose us before the foundation of the world is both humbling and awe-inspiring. This divine choice is often referred to as predestination, a concept that highlights God's sovereignty and His overarching plan for humanity. Predestination means that our salvation and identity as God's children are not accidents of history but part of His eternal purpose.

1. God's Sovereignty: God's choice of us underscores His sovereign control over all things. Before we were born, before the world even existed, God had a plan for us. This truth gives us confidence that our lives are not random but part of a divine design.

2. Beyond Human Understanding: The mystery of predestination is beyond full human comprehension. We may struggle to understand why God chooses some and not others, but we can trust that His decisions are based on His perfect wisdom, justice, and love.

The Unconditional Love of God

Ephesians 1:4-5 emphasizes that God's choice of us is grounded in His love. This love is unconditional, not based on our performance or worthiness. It is a pure, self-giving love that seeks our highest good.

1. Love as the Basis: God's love is the foundation of His choice. He chose us not because we were deserving but because He is loving. This love is the same that compelled Him to send Jesus to die for our sins (John 3:16).

2. Security in God's Love: Knowing that we are loved unconditionally by God gives us a secure foundation for our

identity. We don't have to earn His love; it is freely given. This security frees us from the fear of rejection and the pressure to perform.

Adoption into God's Family

One of the most beautiful aspects of being chosen by God is our adoption into His family. Ephesians 1:5 states that God predestined us for adoption to sonship through Jesus Christ. This adoption is a profound transformation of our identity and status.

1. From Orphans to Children: Spiritually, we were once orphans—separated from God and without hope. Through Christ, we have been adopted into God's family. This adoption gives us the rights and privileges of children, including access to God as our Father (Romans 8:15).

2. Heirs with Christ: As adopted children, we are also heirs with Christ. This means we share in His inheritance, which includes eternal life, the indwelling of the Holy Spirit, and the promise of future glory (Romans 8:17).

Holy and Blameless

God chose us to be holy and blameless in His sight. This calling is both a privilege and a responsibility. Holiness involves being set apart for God's purposes, and living in a way that reflects His character.

1. Set Apart: To be holy means to be set apart from sin and dedicated to God. This involves a daily commitment to live according to His standards and values, rather than those of the world.

2. Blameless: Being blameless means living in integrity and righteousness. It doesn't imply perfection but a sincere pursuit of God's will and a willingness to repent when we fall short.

Living Out Our Identity

Understanding that we are chosen and beloved by God transforms how we live. It gives us a sense of purpose and direction, knowing that our lives are part of a divine plan.

1. Purposeful Living: Our identity as chosen and beloved children of God gives us a clear purpose. We are called to live in a way that honors Him, reflecting His love and holiness to the world.

2. Empowered by Grace: God's grace empowers us to live out our calling. We are not left to our own devices but have the Holy Spirit within us, guiding and strengthening us (Ephesians 3:16).

The Response of Gratitude

Our response to being chosen and beloved by God should be one of gratitude and worship. Recognizing the depth of God's love and grace compels us to live lives of thankfulness.

1. Worship: Gratitude naturally leads to worship. We praise God for His incredible love and the privilege of being His children. Worship becomes a central part of our lives as we express our love and adoration for Him.

2. Service: Gratitude also motivates us to serve others. As recipients of God's love and grace, we are called to extend that love to those around us, serving them selflessly and sacrificially.

In conclusion, understanding that we are chosen and beloved by God is a transformative truth. It gives us a secure identity, a sense of purpose, and a calling to live holy and blameless lives. As we embrace this identity and respond with gratitude and worship, we fulfill God's divine plan for our lives, bringing glory to Him and experiencing the fullness of His love.

CHAPTER 03

REDEEMED AND RESTORED

1 Peter 2:9: "But you are a chosen people, a royal priesthood, a holy nation, God's special possession, that you may declare the praises of him who called you out of darkness into his wonderful light."

Through the sacrifice of Jesus Christ, we have been redeemed and restored to a right relationship with God. Our past sins and failures no longer define us. Instead, we are now part of God's royal priesthood, called to live in the light and share His love with the world. This redemption is a continuous process of transformation, making us more like Christ each day.

The Nature of Redemption

Redemption is a central theme in the Bible, illustrating God's profound love and mercy towards humanity. To redeem means to buy back, to liberate, or to restore. In the context of our faith, redemption refers to Jesus Christ's sacrificial death on the cross, which paid the price for our sins and freed us from the bondage of sin and death.

1. The Price of Redemption: Jesus paid the ultimate price for our redemption with His blood. His death was a substitutionary sacrifice, taking upon Himself the punishment that we deserved (1 Peter 1:18-19). This act of love and grace was necessary to satisfy God's justice and to restore us to a right relationship with Him.

2. The Result of Redemption: Through Christ's sacrifice, we are forgiven and set free. Our sins are washed away, and we are no longer slaves to sin. Instead, we are given a new identity as children of God, with the promise of eternal life (Ephesians 1:7).

Restoration to a Right Relationship

Redemption is not just about being forgiven; it also involves being restored to a right relationship with God. This restoration is both a one-time event and an ongoing process.

1. Justification: At the moment of our salvation, we are justified—declared righteous before God. This legal declaration means that our sins are forgiven, and we are clothed in the righteousness of Christ (Romans 5:1). Justification restores our relationship with God, making us His beloved children.

2. Sanctification: While justification is a one-time event, sanctification is a lifelong process. Sanctification involves being made holy, and becoming more like Christ in our thoughts, attitudes, and actions. This process is the work of the Holy Spirit, who empowers us to live out our new identity (Philippians 2:12-13).

A Royal Priesthood

1 Peter 2:9 describes believers as a royal priesthood. This imagery is rich with meaning, drawing from Old Testament concepts and applying them to the New Testament church.

1. Priestly Role: In the Old Testament, priests were mediators between God and the people, offering sacrifices and interceding on behalf of the nation. As believers, we are called to a similar role, interceding for others and offering spiritual sacrifices, such as praise, prayer, and acts of service (Hebrews 13:15-16).

2. Royal Identity: Being part of a royal priesthood means that we share in the kingship of Christ. We are co-heirs with Him, destined to reign with Him in His eternal kingdom (Romans 8:17). This royal identity gives us a sense of dignity and purpose, knowing that we are God's special possession.

Called Out of Darkness

Our redemption involves being called out of darkness into God's wonderful light. This metaphor highlights the dramatic change that occurs when we come to faith in Christ.

1. From Darkness to Light: Darkness represents sin, ignorance, and separation from God. Light symbolizes truth, holiness, and communion with God. When we are redeemed, we are transferred from the kingdom of darkness to the kingdom of light (Colossians 1:13).

2. Living in the Light: As children of the light, we are called to live differently. This means rejecting sinful behaviors and embracing a lifestyle that reflects God's character. We are to shine as lights in a dark world, demonstrating the love and truth of Christ (Ephesians 5:8-9).

Declaring His Praises

A key aspect of our new identity is to declare the praises of Him who called us out of darkness. Our redemption is not just for our benefit but for the glory of God. We are to be witnesses of His grace and goodness.

1. Proclaiming the Gospel: Declaring God's praises involves sharing the gospel with others. We are called to testify to the transformative power of Christ in our lives and invite others to experience the same redemption (Matthew 28:19-20).

2. Worship and Gratitude: Our lives should be marked by worship and gratitude. We praise God not only with our words but with our actions, living in a way that honors Him and reflects His love (Psalm 34:1-3).

Continuous Transformation

Redemption is a continuous process of transformation, making us more like Christ each day. This ongoing work of sanctification requires our active participation and cooperation with the Holy Spirit.

1. Renewing the Mind: Transformation begins with the renewal of our minds. As we immerse ourselves in God's Word and align our thinking with His truth, we are transformed from the inside out (Romans 12:2).

2. Growing in Holiness: Sanctification involves growing in holiness, which means setting ourselves apart for God's purposes and living in obedience to His commands. This growth is a gradual process, marked by daily choices to follow Christ (1 Thessalonians 4:3-4).

3. Bearing Fruit: As we abide in Christ, we bear fruit that reflects His character. This includes the fruit of the Spirit—love, joy, peace, patience, kindness, goodness, faithfulness, gentleness, and self-control (Galatians 5:22-23). Bearing fruit is evidence of our ongoing transformation and a testimony to God's work in our lives.

In conclusion, our redemption and restoration through Jesus Christ are profound and transformative. We are no longer defined by our past sins and failures but are now part of God's royal priesthood, called to live in the light and declare His praises. This redemption is a continuous process of transformation, making us more like Christ each day. As we embrace our new identity and live out our calling, we experience the fullness of God's love and grace, bringing glory to Him and hope to the world.

CHAPTER 04

LIVING AS GOD'S PEOPLE

Romans 12:1-2: "Therefore, I urge you, brothers and sisters, in view of God's mercy, to offer your bodies as a living sacrifice, holy and pleasing to God—this is your true and proper worship. Do not conform to the pattern of this world, but be transformed by the renewing of your mind. Then you will be able to test and approve what God's will is—his good, pleasing, and perfect will."

As people who belong to God, our lives should reflect His holiness and love. This involves offering ourselves as living sacrifices, fully committed to His purposes. By renewing our minds through God's Word and resisting conformity to worldly values, we can discern and fulfill God's will for our lives. This transformation affects every aspect of our being, leading us to live out our faith authentically and powerfully.

Living Sacrifices

Paul begins Romans 12 with a powerful exhortation to present our bodies as living sacrifices. This concept is deeply rooted in the sacrificial system of the Old Testament, where animals were offered to God as an act of worship. However, in the New Testament, the call is for a different kind of sacrifice—one that involves our entire being.

1. Total Commitment: Offering ourselves as living sacrifices means a total commitment to God. It involves surrendering every part of our lives—our thoughts, actions, desires, and ambitions—to His control. This level of commitment is a response to God's mercy, recognizing that He has given everything for us.

2. Holy and Pleasing to God: The sacrifices we offer are to be holy and pleasing to God. Holiness involves being set apart for God's purposes, and living in a way that honors Him. Our lives should reflect His character and bring delight to Him.

3. True Worship: True worship is not limited to singing songs or attending church services. It is a lifestyle of dedication to God. When we offer ourselves as living sacrifices, our daily actions, choices, and attitudes become acts of worship, glorifying God in all that we do.

Renewing the Mind

Transformation begins with the renewal of our minds. The mind is the battleground where spiritual transformation takes place. By changing the way we think, we align ourselves with God's truth and resist the pressures of the world.

1. Resisting Conformity: Paul urges believers not to conform to the pattern of this world. The world has its own values, priorities, and ways of thinking, often contrary to God's will. As God's people, we are called to stand apart from these worldly influences and live according to His standards.

2. Renewing the Mind: The process of renewing our minds involves immersing ourselves in God's Word. Scripture is the primary means through which our minds are transformed. By studying, meditating on, and applying God's Word, we replace worldly thinking with divine truth.

3. Testing and Approving God's Will: As our minds are renewed, we gain the ability to discern God's will. This discernment allows us to test and approve what is good, pleasing, and perfect in His sight. Knowing and doing God's will becomes our guiding principle, leading us to live lives that honor Him.

Living Out Holiness

Holiness is a central aspect of living as God's people. It involves being set apart for God's purposes and reflecting

His character in our daily lives. Holiness is not about perfection but about a sincere pursuit of godliness.

1. Personal Conduct: Holiness affects our personal conduct. It means avoiding sin and striving for purity in our thoughts, words, and actions. We are called to be holy because God is holy (1 Peter 1:15-16).

2. Relationships: Holiness extends to our relationships. We are to love others as God loves us, showing kindness, compassion, and forgiveness. Our interactions should reflect the grace and mercy we have received from God.

3. Integrity: Living out holiness requires integrity. We are to be people of honesty, reliability, and moral uprightness. Our actions should align with our beliefs, demonstrating the authenticity of our faith.

Living Out Love

Love is the defining mark of a follower of Christ. Jesus commanded His disciples to love one another as He has loved them (John 13:34-35). Living as God's people means embodying this love in every aspect of our lives.

1. Sacrificial Love: Jesus' love for us was sacrificial, demonstrated most profoundly on the cross. We are called to love others with this same selfless, sacrificial love, putting their needs above our own (1 John 3:16).

2. Love in Action: Love is more than a feeling; it is action. It involves tangible expressions of care and compassion. We are to serve others, meet their needs, and seek their well-being (James 2:14-17).

3. Love for Enemies: Jesus taught us to love our enemies and pray for those who persecute us (Matthew 5:44). This radical love sets us apart from the world and reflects the transformative power of God's grace.

Living Out Transformation

Transformation is an ongoing process. It involves daily decisions to follow Christ and allow the Holy Spirit to work in us. This transformation affects every area of our lives, making us more like Christ.

1. Daily Renewal: Transformation requires daily renewal. We must continually seek God, immerse ourselves in His Word, and allow the Holy Spirit to guide us. This ongoing renewal keeps us aligned with God's purposes.

2. Spiritual Disciplines: Spiritual disciplines such as prayer, fasting, and worship are essential for transformation. These practices draw us closer to God and strengthen our faith, enabling us to live out our identity as His people.

3. Community: Transformation is also fostered within the community of believers. The church provides support, accountability, and encouragement as we grow in our faith.

Being part of a spiritual family helps us stay committed to God's will.

Discernment and Fulfillment of God's Will

Living as God's people involves discerning and fulfilling His will. This requires a deep relationship with God and a sensitivity to His leading.

1. Prayerful Discernment: Discernment begins with prayer. We must seek God's guidance in every decision, trusting that He will direct our paths (Proverbs 3:5-6). Prayer keeps us connected to God's heart and aligns our desires with His.

2. Obedience: Knowing God's will is only the first step; we must also obey it. Obedience demonstrates our love for God and our commitment to His purposes. It involves trusting His wisdom, even when His ways are not clear to us.

3. Faith and Action: Discerning and fulfilling God's will requires faith and action. We must step out in faith, confident that God is with us and will empower us to accomplish His purposes. Our actions should reflect our trust in Him and our desire to glorify Him.

In conclusion, living as God's people involves offering ourselves as living sacrifices, renewing our minds through His Word, and resisting conformity to worldly values. It means living out holiness, love, and transformation in every aspect of our lives. By discerning and fulfilling God's will, we glorify Him and experience the fullness of His purpose for us. As we embrace this calling, we become powerful witnesses of His grace and truth, shining as lights in a dark world.

CHAPTER 05

OUR IDENTITY IN CHRIST

Galatians 2:20: "I have been crucified with Christ and I no longer live, but Christ lives in me. The life I now live in the body, I live by faith in the Son of God, who loved me and gave himself for me."

Our identity is now in Christ. His life, death, and resurrection define who we are. We are no longer slaves to sin but are free to live by faith, empowered by His Spirit. This new identity calls us to a higher standard of living, reflecting the character of Christ in our daily interactions and decisions.

Crucified with Christ

The Apostle Paul begins Galatians 2:20 with a profound declaration: "I have been crucified with Christ." This statement signifies a fundamental transformation that occurs when we come to faith in Jesus. It speaks to the radical change in our identity and the new life we receive in Him.

1. Death to the Old Self: Being crucified with Christ means that our old self, with its sinful desires and tendencies, has been put to death. This is a spiritual reality that takes place at the moment of our conversion. Our old identity, rooted in sin and separation from God, is crucified with Christ on the cross (Romans 6:6).

2. Union with Christ: Our crucifixion with Christ also signifies our union with Him. We are united with Jesus in His death, burial, and resurrection. This union means that His victory over sin and death becomes our victory, and His life becomes our life (Romans 6:4-5).

Christ Lives in Me

Paul continues, "But Christ lives in me." This truth is at the heart of our new identity in Christ. The indwelling presence of Jesus transforms our lives and empowers us to live according to His will.

1. Indwelling Presence: Christ's indwelling presence is the source of our new life. Through the Holy Spirit, Jesus lives within us, guiding, teaching, and empowering us. This intimate relationship with Christ is the foundation of our identity and our strength for daily living (John 14:17, 23).

2. Transformative Power: The presence of Christ in us is transformative. It changes our desires, attitudes, and behaviors. As we yield to His Spirit, we become more like Him, reflecting His character in our interactions and decisions (2 Corinthians 3:18).

Living by Faith

Paul declares, "The life I now live in the body, I live by faith in the Son of God." Living by faith is central to our new identity in Christ. It involves trusting Jesus daily and relying on His grace and power.

1. Faith in Christ: Living by faith means placing our trust in Jesus for every aspect of our lives. It is a daily decision to rely on His wisdom, strength, and provision. Faith is not merely intellectual assent but a deep, abiding trust in the person and work of Christ (Hebrews 11:1).

2. Walking in the Spirit: Living by faith also means walking in the Spirit. The Holy Spirit guides us, empowers us, and produces fruit in our lives. As we walk in the Spirit, we are led by God and empowered to live out our identity in Christ (Galatians 5:16-25).

Loved and Empowered

Paul emphasizes the motivation for his new life: "who loved me and gave himself for me." Our identity in Christ is rooted in His sacrificial love and the empowerment that comes from His Spirit.

1. The Love of Christ: Jesus' love for us is the foundation of our identity. His sacrificial death on the cross demonstrates the depth of His love and the extent of His commitment to us. This love defines who we are and gives us a sense of worth and purpose (Ephesians 3:17-19).

2. Empowered by His Spirit: The Holy Spirit empowers us to live out our new identity in Christ. He equips us with spiritual gifts, strengthens us in our weaknesses, and guides us in all truth. This empowerment enables us to fulfill God's purposes and live victoriously (Acts 1:8).

Higher Standard of Living

Our new identity in Christ calls us to a higher standard of living. We are no longer slaves to sin but are called to live holy and righteous lives, reflecting the character of Christ.

1. Freedom from Sin: In Christ, we are set free from the power of sin. This freedom is not an excuse for licentiousness but a call to live in righteousness. We are empowered to resist temptation and to pursue holiness (Romans 6:18-22).

2. Reflecting Christ's Character: Our lives should reflect the character of Christ. This involves growing in virtues such as love, joy, peace, patience, kindness, goodness,

faithfulness, gentleness, and self-control. As we grow in these areas, we become more like Jesus and a testimony of His transforming power (Galatians 5:22-23).

3. Living with Purpose: Our identity in Christ gives us a clear purpose. We are called to be His ambassadors, representing Him in the world. This involves sharing the gospel, serving others, and living in a way that brings glory to God (2 Corinthians 5:20).

Daily Application

Living out our identity in Christ requires daily application. It is a continual process of growth and transformation, involving practical steps that help us align our lives with His will.

1. Daily Surrender: Each day, we must surrender our will to God, asking Him to lead us and empower us. This involves prayer, seeking His guidance, and committing to follow His direction.

2. Immersing in Scripture: God's Word is essential for understanding our identity in Christ and for guiding our lives. We must immerse ourselves in Scripture, studying, meditating, and applying its truths.

3. Community and Accountability: Being part of a Christian community provides support, encouragement, and

accountability. Fellow believers help us stay committed to our faith and grow in our walk with Christ.

4. Serving Others: Serving others is a practical way to live out our identity in Christ. As we serve, we demonstrate His love and reflect His character. Service also helps us develop humility and compassion.

Our identity in Christ is a profound and transformative reality. We are crucified with Christ, and He lives in us. We live by faith in the Son of God, who loved us and gave Himself for us. This new identity calls us to a higher standard of living, reflecting the character of Christ in our daily interactions and decisions. As we embrace our identity in Him, we experience the fullness of His love and power, and we become powerful witnesses of His grace to the world.

Living out our identity in Christ is a lifelong journey. It requires continual growth, daily surrender, and a deep reliance on the Holy Spirit. As we walk this path, we become more like Jesus, bringing glory to God and advancing His kingdom on earth. May we live each day in the fullness of our identity in Christ, empowered by His Spirit, and motivated by His love.

CHAPTER 06

THE FAMILY OF GOD

1 John 3:1: "See what great love the Father has lavished on us, that we should be called children of God! And that is what we are! The reason the world does not know us is that it did not know him."

Being part of God's family is one of the greatest privileges we can have. As His children, we are loved, valued, and protected. This familial relationship also brings responsibilities: to love one another, support each other, and work together for God's kingdom. Understanding our place in God's family encourages us to build deep, meaningful relationships within the church community.

The Love of the Father

John's declaration in 1 John 3:1 emphasizes the greatness of God's love. This love is the foundation of our identity as His children. It is a love that surpasses understanding and is lavished upon us, not because of anything we have done, but because of who God is.

1. Lavish Love: God's love is extravagant and abundant. It is not given sparingly but poured out generously upon us. This love is unconditional, based on God's nature rather than our merit (Ephesians 2:4-5).

2. Adoption into God's Family: Through this great love, we are adopted into God's family. Adoption is a legal act that changes our status and gives us a new identity. We are no longer slaves to sin but are now beloved children of God (Romans 8:15-17).

3. Security in God's Love: As God's children, we are secure in His love. This security gives us confidence and peace, knowing that nothing can separate us from His love (Romans 8:38-39).

The Privileges of Being God's Children

Being part of God's family comes with incredible privileges. These privileges reflect our new identity and the special relationship we have with God.

1. Loved and Valued: As God's children, we are deeply loved and valued. This love is not based on our performance

but on our relationship with Him. We can rest in the assurance that we are precious in His sight (Zephaniah 3:17).

2. Protected and Provided For: God, as our Father, promises to protect and provide for us. He cares for our needs and watches over us with a loving and attentive eye (Matthew 6:25-34).

3. Heirs with Christ: As children of God, we are also heirs with Christ. This means we share in His inheritance, including eternal life and the blessings of His kingdom (Galatians 4:7).

The Responsibilities of Being God's Children

With the privileges of being God's children come responsibilities. These responsibilities involve how we relate to one another within the family of God and how we live out our faith.

1. Loving One Another: Jesus commanded His disciples to love one another as He has loved them (John 13:34-35). This love is the hallmark of being part of God's family. It involves selfless, sacrificial love that seeks the best for others.

2. Supporting Each Other: Being part of God's family means we are not alone. We are called to support and encourage one another, bearing each other's burdens and helping each other grow in faith (Galatians 6:2).

3. Working Together for God's Kingdom: As God's children, we have a collective mission to advance His kingdom. This involves using our gifts and talents to serve the church and reach out to the world with the gospel (1 Corinthians 12:12-27).

Building Deep, Meaningful Relationships

Understanding our place in God's family encourages us to build deep, meaningful relationships within the church community. These relationships are vital for our spiritual growth and for the health of the church.

1. Fellowship: Fellowship is more than just socializing; it is a deep connection with other believers based on our shared faith in Christ. This fellowship involves mutual support, accountability, and encouragement (Acts 2:42).

2. Unity: Unity is essential in the family of God. We are called to be united in love, purpose, and mission. This unity reflects the oneness of the Trinity and is a powerful witness to the world (Ephesians 4:3-6).

3. Forgiveness and Reconciliation: As members of God's family, we must practice forgiveness and seek reconciliation. This involves resolving conflicts, extending grace, and maintaining harmony within the church (Colossians 3:13).

Living Out Our Family Identity

Living out our identity as God's family involves practical steps that demonstrate our love and commitment to one another.

1. Hospitality: Hospitality is a tangible way to show love and build relationships. It involves opening our homes and hearts to others, and creating a welcoming and inclusive environment (1 Peter 4:9).

2. Serving One Another: Serving one another is a practical expression of our love. This can involve meeting physical needs, offering emotional support, and helping each other grow spiritually (Galatians 5:13).

3. Praying for Each Other: Prayer is a powerful way to support one another. We are called to pray for each other's needs, struggles, and spiritual growth, trusting that God hears and answers our prayers (James 5:16).

Reflecting God's Love to the World

As God's family, we are called to reflect His love to the world. This involves living out the gospel in our daily lives and being a light in a dark world.

1. Being Witnesses: Our lives should testify to the love and grace of God. This involves sharing the gospel through our words and actions, pointing others to Christ (Matthew 5:14-16).

2. Showing Compassion: We are called to show compassion to those in need, reflecting the heart of our Father. This includes acts of kindness, mercy, and justice (Micah 6:8).

3. Living Distinctly: As children of God, we are called to live distinctly from the world. This means living according to God's standards and values, even when they differ from societal norms (Romans 12:2).

Being part of God's family is a profound privilege and a great responsibility. We are loved, valued, and protected by our heavenly Father. As His children, we are called to love one another, support each other, and work together for His kingdom. Understanding our place in God's family encourages us to build deep, meaningful relationships within the church community and to reflect His love to the world. May we live out our identity as God's family, bringing glory to Him and advancing His kingdom on earth.

CHAPTER 07

OUR INHERITANCE

Romans 8:17: "Now if we are children, then we are heirs—heirs of God and co-heirs with Christ, if indeed we share in his sufferings in order that we may also share in his glory."

As God's children, we have a glorious inheritance. This inheritance includes eternal life, the indwelling of the Holy Spirit, and the promise of being with God forever. While we may face trials and sufferings in this world, these are temporary and pale in comparison to the eternal glory that awaits us. Our inheritance gives us hope and motivates us to persevere in our faith.

The Nature of Our Inheritance

Our inheritance as God's children is multifaceted and surpasses anything we can imagine. It encompasses both present realities and future promises, offering us profound hope and encouragement.

1. Eternal Life: One of the most significant aspects of our inheritance is eternal life. This is not just an unending existence but a quality of life that begins now and extends into eternity. Eternal life is characterized by an intimate relationship with God, knowing Him, and being known by Him (John 17:3).

2. Indwelling of the Holy Spirit: As believers, we are given the Holy Spirit as a deposit guaranteeing our inheritance (Ephesians 1:13-14). The Holy Spirit empowers us, guides us into all truth, and transforms us into the likeness of Christ. His presence in our lives is a foretaste of the full inheritance we will receive.

3. The Promise of Being with God Forever: Our ultimate inheritance is being with God forever. This promise assures us that we will dwell in His presence, experiencing His love, peace, and joy without end. Revelation 21:3-4 describes the beauty of this inheritance: "They will be his people, and God himself will be with them and be their God. 'He will wipe every tear from their eyes. There will be no more death or mourning or crying or pain, for the old order of things has passed away."

Sharing in Christ's Sufferings and Glory

Romans 8:17 highlights a vital truth: as heirs of God and co-heirs with Christ, we share in both His sufferings and His glory. This dual reality shapes our understanding of the Christian life and our inheritance.

1. Sharing in His Sufferings: Following Christ involves suffering. Jesus Himself warned that in this world we would have trouble (John 16:33). Suffering can take many forms, including persecution, trials, and personal struggles. However, these sufferings are not meaningless. They have a purpose in God's plan, refining our faith and drawing us closer to Him (1 Peter 1:6-7).

2. Sharing in His Glory: The sufferings of this present time are not worth comparing with the glory that will be revealed in us (Romans 8:18). Sharing in Christ's glory means we will be glorified with Him, transformed into His likeness, and fully reflecting His character. This future glory far outweighs any temporary trials we face.

The Hope of Our Inheritance

Our inheritance gives us hope—a confident expectation of future blessings that sustain us through difficult times. This hope is anchored in God's promises and the finished work of Christ.

1. A Living Hope: Our hope is living because it is based on the resurrection of Jesus Christ from the dead (1

Peter 1:3). His victory over death guarantees our inheritance and assures us that nothing can separate us from God's love (Romans 8:38-39).

2. Motivation to Persevere: The hope of our inheritance motivates us to persevere in our faith. Knowing that our present sufferings are temporary and that eternal glory awaits us encourages us to remain steadfast, even in the face of adversity (2 Corinthians 4:16-18).

3. Joy in Trials: Our inheritance allows us to find joy even in trials. James 1:2-4 urges us to consider it pure joy when we face trials of many kinds because they produce perseverance, maturity, and completeness in our faith. The hope of our inheritance gives us perspective, enabling us to see trials as opportunities for growth.

Living in Light of Our Inheritance

Understanding our inheritance shapes how we live in the present. It calls us to a higher standard of living and a deeper commitment to God's purposes.

1. Living as Heirs: As heirs of God, we are called to live in a manner worthy of our inheritance. This means pursuing holiness, integrity, and love. Our lives should reflect the values of God's kingdom and serve as a testimony to His grace (Ephesians 4:1).

2. Investing in Eternity: Our inheritance encourages us to invest in things that have eternal value. This includes sharing the gospel, serving others, and growing in our relationship with God. Jesus taught that we should store up treasures in heaven, where they will not be destroyed (Matthew 6:19-21).

3. Encouraging One Another: The hope of our inheritance should lead us to encourage and build up one another. We are part of a spiritual family, and we need each other's support to remain faithful. Hebrews 10:24-25 exhorts us to spur one another on toward love and good deeds and to meet together regularly for mutual encouragement.

The Eternal Perspective

Our inheritance gives us an eternal perspective, helping us to focus on what truly matters. This perspective shapes our priorities, decisions, and actions.

1. Living with Purpose: Knowing that we have an eternal inheritance gives our lives purpose. We are not aimlessly drifting but are part of God's grand plan. This purpose drives us to live intentionally, making choices that align with His will (Colossians 3:23-24).

2. Overcoming Fear: The certainty of our inheritance helps us overcome fear. We do not need to fear the future,

suffering, or even death because we know that our ultimate destiny is secure in Christ (Psalm 27:1).

3. Anticipating Glory: The hope of our inheritance fills us with anticipation for the future. We look forward to the day when we will fully experience God's glory and be reunited with Him. This anticipation brings joy and inspires us to live faithfully in the present (1 Thessalonians 4:16-18).

In conclusion, our inheritance as God's children is a glorious and multifaceted blessing. It includes eternal life, the indwelling of the Holy Spirit, and the promise of being with God forever. While we may face trials and sufferings in this world, these are temporary and pale in comparison to the eternal glory that awaits us. Our inheritance gives us hope and motivates us to persevere in our faith. As we live in light of this inheritance, we are called to a higher standard of living, investing in eternity, and encouraging one another. May the hope of our inheritance fill us with joy, purpose, and a deep sense of God's love, as we anticipate the day when we will fully share in His glory.

CHAPTER 08

AMBASSADORS FOR CHRIST

2 Corinthians 5:20: "We are therefore Christ's ambassadors, as though God were making his appeal through us. We implore you on Christ's behalf: Be reconciled to God."

As God's people, we are called to be His ambassadors, representing Christ to the world. This involves sharing the message of reconciliation and living out the gospel in our actions. Our lives should reflect the love, grace, and truth of Jesus, drawing others to Him. Being an ambassador for Christ is both a privilege and a responsibility, requiring us to live with integrity and purpose.

The Role of an Ambassador

An ambassador is a representative who acts on behalf of someone else, carrying their message and authority. As ambassadors for Christ, we represent Him to the world, entrusted with the ministry of reconciliation.

1. Representing Christ: As Christ's ambassadors, we are His representatives on earth. This means that in our words, actions, and attitudes, we reflect who Jesus is. People should be able to see Christ in us and be drawn to Him through our lives (John 13:35).

2. Carrying His Message: The primary message we carry as ambassadors is the message of reconciliation. God has reconciled the world to Himself through Christ, and He has entrusted us with the message of this reconciliation. Our mission is to implore others to be reconciled to God, sharing the good news of Jesus' sacrificial love and forgiveness (2 Corinthians 5:18-19).

The Message of Reconciliation

Reconciliation is the heart of the gospel. It involves restoring a broken relationship between God and humanity. Our role as ambassadors is to communicate this message clearly and compellingly.

1. The Need for Reconciliation: Humanity is separated from God because of sin. This separation results in spiritual death and alienation from the Creator. The message of reconciliation addresses this fundamental problem by offering a solution through Jesus Christ (Romans 3:23, 6:23).

2. The Means of Reconciliation: Reconciliation is made possible through the life, death, and resurrection of Jesus. He took upon Himself the punishment for our sins, satisfying God's justice and making it possible for us to be restored to a right relationship with Him (1 Peter 3:18).

3. The Response to Reconciliation: The message of reconciliation calls for a response. It invites people to turn from their sins, trust in Jesus, and enter into a restored relationship with God. Our role as ambassadors is to extend this invitation and urge others to accept it (Acts 3:19).

Living Out the Gospel

Being an ambassador for Christ is not just about what we say; it's also about how we live. Our lives should be a living testimony of the gospel, reflecting the character and love of Jesus.

1. Integrity: Living with integrity is essential for an ambassador. Integrity involves being honest, trustworthy, and consistent in our actions. As we live with integrity, we demonstrate the truth of the gospel and build credibility with those we seek to reach (Proverbs 11:3).

2. Grace: Our lives should be marked by grace. This means extending kindness, forgiveness, and love to others, even when they do not deserve it. Grace is a powerful

testimony of God's love and can open hearts to the message of reconciliation (Ephesians 4:32).

3. Truth: As ambassadors, we must stand for truth. This involves upholding biblical principles and speaking the truth in love. While it may be challenging, being committed to truth is crucial for faithfully representing Christ (Ephesians 4:15).

The Privilege of Being an Ambassador

Being an ambassador for Christ is a profound privilege. It is an honor to be chosen by God to represent Him and to carry His message of reconciliation to the world.

1. Chosen by God: We have been chosen by God for this role. This selection is not based on our merit but on His grace. Being chosen as His ambassador should fill us with gratitude and a sense of responsibility (John 15:16).

2. Empowered by the Spirit: God does not leave us to fulfill this role in our strength. He empowers us through the Holy Spirit, giving us the wisdom, boldness, and love we need to be effective ambassadors (Acts 1:8).

3. Part of His Plan: As ambassadors, we are part of God's redemptive plan. Our efforts in sharing the gospel and living out our faith contribute to His kingdom's purposes. This perspective gives our lives eternal significance and purpose (2 Corinthians 5:20-21).

The Responsibility of Being an Ambassador

With the privilege of being an ambassador comes great responsibility. We are accountable to God for how we represent Him and steward the message of reconciliation.

1. Faithfulness: We must be faithful in our role as ambassadors. This involves being diligent in sharing the gospel, consistent in our walk with Christ, and committed to living out His commands. Faithfulness in small things can lead to greater opportunities to impact others for Christ (Matthew 25:21).

2. Courage: Being an ambassador requires courage. We may face opposition, rejection, or persecution, but we are called to stand firm and boldly proclaim the gospel. Our courage comes from knowing that God is with us and that His message has the power to change lives (Joshua 1:9).

3. Compassion: Our role as ambassadors must be marked by compassion. We are called to reach out to the lost, the hurting, and the broken with the love of Christ. Compassionate actions and words can soften hearts and open doors for the gospel (Matthew 9:36).

Practical Steps for Being an Effective Ambassador

To be effective ambassadors for Christ, we need to take practical steps that align our lives with our calling.

1. Pray for Opportunities: Pray for God to open doors for you to share the gospel and to give you the boldness to speak when those opportunities arise. Prayer is essential for preparing our hearts and for God to work in the hearts of those we encounter (Colossians 4:3-4).

2. Live Out Your Faith: Let your life be a testimony of God's grace. Live with integrity, show kindness and compassion, and strive to reflect Christ in all you do. Your actions can speak volumes and attract others to the message you carry (1 Peter 2:12).

3. Build Relationships: Invest in relationships with people who do not know Christ. Build trust, listen to their stories, and share your faith naturally within the context of genuine friendships. Relational evangelism is often more effective than impersonal approaches (John 4:7-26).

4. Share Your Story: Be prepared to share your personal testimony of how Christ has changed your life. Your story is unique and powerful and can resonate with others in ways that abstract concepts cannot (1 Peter 3:15).

5. Equip Yourself: Equip yourself with knowledge of the Bible and understanding of the gospel. Be ready to answer questions and address doubts with gentleness and respect. Ongoing discipleship and study of God's Word will

strengthen your ability to represent Him well (2 Timothy 2:15).

As ambassadors for Christ, we have the incredible privilege and responsibility of representing Him to the world. We carry the message of reconciliation, living out the gospel through our words and actions. Our lives should reflect the love, grace, and truth of Jesus, drawing others to Him. By living with integrity and purpose, we fulfill our calling as His representatives, bringing glory to God and advancing His kingdom. May we embrace this role with joy and dedication, knowing that God has chosen and empowered us for this vital mission.

CHAPTER 09

THE POWER OF UNITY

Ephesians 4:3-6: "Make every effort to keep the unity of the Spirit through the bond of peace. There is one body and one Spirit, just as you were called to one hope when you were called; one Lord, one faith, one baptism; one God and Father of all, who is over all and through all and in all."

Unity among God's people is essential. It reflects the oneness of God and strengthens our witness to the world. By embracing our shared faith and working together in love, we can accomplish much for God's kingdom. Unity requires humility, patience, and a willingness to prioritize the common good over personal preferences.

The Foundation of Unity

Unity in the body of Christ is founded on the fundamental truths of our faith. These truths provide the basis for our oneness and guide our efforts to maintain unity.

1. One Body: The church is described as one body with many members (1 Corinthians 12:12-14). This metaphor emphasizes our interconnectedness and mutual dependence. Each member has a unique role, but all work together for the health and growth of the body.

2. One Spirit: The Holy Spirit unites us as believers. He dwells within each of us, guiding, empowering, and equipping us for service. The Spirit's presence ensures that we are not operating in our strength but in God's power (Ephesians 4:4).

3. One Hope: Our shared hope in Christ binds us together. This hope encompasses our present salvation and our future glory with God. It is a source of encouragement and motivation, reminding us that we are on the same journey (Ephesians 4:4).

4. One Lord, One Faith, One Baptism: We acknowledge one Lord—Jesus Christ—whose lordship we all submit to. Our faith in Him is the basis of our unity, and baptism symbolizes our identification with Him and with one another (Ephesians 4:5).

5. One God and Father: God the Father is the ultimate source of our unity. He is overall, through all, and in all, providing a unifying presence that transcends our differences (Ephesians 4:6).

The Attitudes that Foster Unity

Maintaining unity requires certain attitudes and behaviors that promote harmony and cooperation among believers.

1. Humility: Humility is essential for unity. It involves recognizing our limitations, valuing others above ourselves, and being willing to serve rather than be served. Humility fosters an environment where others feel respected and valued (Philippians 2:3-4).

2. Gentleness: Gentleness involves treating others with kindness and consideration, even when there are disagreements. It is the opposite of harshness and aggression, promoting peace and understanding (Galatians 6:1).

3. Patience: Patience is vital for maintaining unity, especially when dealing with differences and conflicts. It involves bearing with one another in love, giving grace for others' shortcomings, and allowing time for growth and change (Colossians 3:12-13).

4. Forgiveness: Forgiveness is crucial for unity. We must be willing to forgive those who wrong us, just as God has forgiven us in Christ. Unforgiveness leads to bitterness and division, while forgiveness restores relationships and fosters unity (Ephesians 4:32).

The Pursuit of Unity

Unity does not happen automatically; it requires intentional effort and commitment. Paul urges us to "make every effort to keep the unity of the Spirit through the bond of peace" (Ephesians 4:3).

1. Pursuing Peace: Peace is the bond that holds unity together. We must actively pursue peace in our relationships, resolving conflicts quickly and seeking reconciliation. This involves being peacemakers, striving to create an environment of harmony and cooperation (Romans 12:18).

2. Valuing Diversity: Unity does not mean uniformity. The body of Christ is diverse, with different gifts, personalities, and backgrounds. We must value and celebrate this diversity, recognizing that it enriches the church and enhances our witness to the world (1 Corinthians 12:4-6).

3. Collaborative Efforts: Working together for God's kingdom requires collaboration and partnership. We must be willing to join forces, share resources, and support one another in ministry. Collaboration amplifies our impact and demonstrates the power of unity (Philippians 1:27).

The Impact of Unity

Unity in the body of Christ has a profound impact on the church and the world. It strengthens our witness, enhances our effectiveness, and brings glory to God.

1. Strengthened Witness: Unity among believers is a powerful testimony to the world. Jesus prayed that His followers would be one so that the world would believe in Him (John 17:20-21). When the church is united, it reflects the love and oneness of God, drawing others to Christ.

2. Enhanced Effectiveness: Unity enhances our effectiveness in ministry. When we work together, we can accomplish more than we could individually. Unity allows us to pool our resources, talents, and efforts for greater impact (Ecclesiastes 4:9-12).

3. Glorifying God: Ultimately, unity brings glory to God. It reflects His nature and fulfills His desire for His people. When the church is united, it honors God and fulfills His purpose for the body of Christ (Romans 15:5-6).

Challenges to Unity

While unity is a divine mandate, it faces many challenges. Understanding these challenges helps us address them effectively.

1. Personal Preferences: Personal preferences can hinder unity. We must be willing to set aside our preferences for the sake of the greater good, prioritizing God's purposes over our desires (Romans 14:19).

2. Misunderstandings and Conflicts: Misunderstandings and conflicts are inevitable in any

community. Addressing them promptly and biblically is essential for maintaining unity. This involves open communication, seeking to understand, and striving for reconciliation (Matthew 18:15-17).

3. Cultural and Theological Differences: Cultural and theological differences can create division. Embracing a spirit of humility and grace helps us navigate these differences, focusing on our shared faith and mission rather than our disagreements (Romans 14:1-3).

Practical Steps to Foster Unity

Fostering unity requires practical steps that build and maintain harmony within the body of Christ.

1. Pray for Unity: Prayer is vital for unity. We must regularly pray for unity within the church, asking God to bind us together in love and purpose. Prayer aligns our hearts with God's desire for unity (John 17:21).

2. Promote Open Communication: Open and honest communication is essential for unity. Encouraging transparency, active listening, and constructive dialogue helps prevent misunderstandings and build trust (Ephesians 4:25).

3. Encourage Participation: Encouraging participation from all members fosters a sense of belonging and ownership. When everyone is involved and valued, it strengthens the unity and health of the church (1 Corinthians 12:14-27).

4. Model Unity: Leaders and mature believers must model unity. Their example sets the tone for the rest of the community. By demonstrating humility, patience, and love, they inspire others to pursue unity (1 Peter 5:3).

The power of unity among God's people cannot be overstated. It reflects the oneness of God, strengthens our witness, and enhances our effectiveness in ministry. By embracing our shared faith and working together in love, we can accomplish much for God's kingdom. Unity requires humility, patience, and a willingness to prioritize the common good over personal preferences. As we make every effort to keep the unity of the Spirit through the bond of peace, we bring glory to God and fulfill His purpose for the body of Christ. May we strive for unity, celebrate our diversity, and work together for the advancement of His kingdom.

CHAPTER 10

OUR ETERNAL HOME

John 14:2-3: "My Father's house has many rooms; if that were not so, would I have told you that I am going there to prepare a place for you? And if I go and prepare a place for you, I will come back and take you to be with me so that you also may be where I am."

Our ultimate destiny is to be with God forever. Jesus has prepared a place for us in His Father's house, and He will return to take us there. This promise of an eternal home fills us with hope and anticipation. It reminds us that our time on earth is temporary and that our true citizenship is in heaven.

The Promise of an Eternal Home

Jesus' words in John 14:2-3 offer profound comfort and hope. He assures us that there is a place prepared for us in His Father's house, and He will come back to take us to be with Him. This promise forms the foundation of our hope and shapes our perspective on life.

1. A Place Prepared: Jesus is preparing a place for us in His Father's house. This assurance means that our eternal home is specifically designed and reserved for us. It speaks to the care and love Jesus has for us, ensuring that we will have a place in His presence (1 Corinthians 2:9).

2. Jesus' Return: The promise of Jesus' return is central to our hope. He will come back to take us to be with Him. This future event is a source of great anticipation for believers, knowing that we will be united with our Savior and live with Him forever (1 Thessalonians 4:16-17).

The Nature of Our Eternal Home

Our eternal home with God is described in various ways throughout Scripture, each providing a glimpse of the glory and joy that awaits us.

1. The Father's House: Jesus refers to our eternal home as His Father's house. This imagery suggests a place of safety, belonging, and familial love. It emphasizes the relational aspect of eternity, where we will dwell in the presence of our loving Father (John 14:2).

2. A New Heaven and New Earth: Revelation 21:1-4 describes a new heaven and a new earth where God will dwell with His people. This renewed creation will be free from pain,

suffering, and death. It will be a place of perfect peace and joy, where God's presence is fully realized.

3. The Holy City: Revelation 21:2-3 speaks of the Holy City, the New Jerusalem, coming down from heaven. This city represents the dwelling place of God with His people, characterized by beauty, holiness, and the absence of sin. It symbolizes the eternal communion we will enjoy with God and one another.

The Certainty of Our Eternal Home

The promise of our eternal home is grounded in the faithfulness of God. His Word assures us of the certainty of this promise, giving us confidence and hope.

1. God's Faithfulness: God is faithful to His promises. He has prepared a place for us, and He will fulfill His promise to bring us to Himself. Our hope is not based on wishful thinking but on the unchanging character of God (Hebrews 10:23).

2. The Resurrection of Jesus: The resurrection of Jesus is the guarantee of our future resurrection and eternal life. Because He lives, we too will live. This historical event provides the foundation for our hope and the assurance of our eternal home (1 Corinthians 15:20-22).

3. The Holy Spirit: The Holy Spirit is given to us as a deposit, guaranteeing our inheritance. His presence in our

lives is a foretaste of the glory to come and a constant reminder of the certainty of our eternal home (Ephesians 1:13-14).

Living in Anticipation

The promise of our eternal home affects how we live in the present. It shapes our values, priorities, and actions, motivating us to live with purpose and hope.

1. Eternal Perspective: Knowing that our time on earth is temporary encourages us to live with an eternal perspective. We are called to set our minds on things above, not on earthly things. This perspective helps us to prioritize what truly matters and to invest in things of eternal significance (Colossians 3:1-2).

2. Holy Living: The anticipation of our eternal home calls us to live holy and godly lives. We are to be diligent in pursuing righteousness, knowing that our ultimate destiny is to be with God. This involves rejecting sin and striving to reflect Christ in all we do (2 Peter 3:11-12).

3. Hope and Endurance: The promise of eternity gives us hope and endurance in the face of trials and suffering. We know that our present difficulties are temporary and that eternal glory awaits us. This hope strengthens us to persevere and remain faithful, even in challenging circumstances (Romans 8:18).

The Joy of Our Eternal Home

Our eternal home is characterized by indescribable joy and fulfillment. It is the culmination of God's redemptive plan and the ultimate realization of His love for us.

1. Fullness of Joy: In God's presence, there is fullness of joy. Our eternal home will be a place of unending delight, where every longing of our hearts is satisfied in Him. The joy of being with God will surpass anything we have experienced on earth (Psalm 16:11).

2. Perfect Fellowship: Our eternal home will be marked by perfect fellowship with God and with one another. We will experience unhindered communion with our Creator and enjoy deep, loving relationships with fellow believers. This fellowship will be a source of great joy and fulfillment (Revelation 21:3-4).

3. Rest and Peace: In our eternal home, we will experience perfect rest and peace. The struggles and burdens of this life will be no more, replaced by the peace of God's presence. This rest is not just physical but a deep, soul-satisfying rest in the love and grace of God (Hebrews 4:9-10).

The Invitation to Our Eternal Home

The promise of our eternal home is extended to all who believe in Jesus Christ. It is an invitation to enter into a relationship with Him and to receive the gift of eternal life.

1. The Gospel Invitation: The gospel is the invitation to our eternal home. It calls us to repent of our sins, trust in Jesus, and follow Him. This invitation is open to all, regardless of background or past mistakes. God's desire is for everyone to come to repentance and to receive the gift of eternal life (John 3:16, 2 Peter 3:9).

2. Responding in Faith: Accepting the invitation to our eternal home requires a response of faith. We must believe in Jesus as our Savior and Lord, trusting in His finished work on the cross. This faith is not merely intellectual assent but a wholehearted commitment to follow Him (Romans 10:9-10).

3. Living with Assurance: Once we have responded to the gospel invitation, we can live with the assurance of our eternal home. This assurance is based on God's promises and the work of Christ. We can have confidence that we belong to Him and that our future is secure (1 John 5:11-13).

The promise of our eternal home fills us with hope and anticipation. Jesus has prepared a place for us in His Father's house, and He will return to take us there. This promise reminds us that our time on earth is temporary and that our true citizenship is in heaven. As we live in anticipation of our eternal home, we are called to live with an eternal perspective, pursuing holiness, and enduring with hope. Our eternal home is characterized by indescribable joy, perfect fellowship, and rest in God's presence. The invitation to this eternal home is extended to all who believe in Jesus Christ. May we embrace this promise, live with the assurance of our eternal home, and eagerly await the day when we will be with God forever.

CHAPTER 11

WALKING IN THE LIGHT

1 John 1:7: "But if we walk in the light, as he is in the light, we have fellowship with one another, and the blood of Jesus, his Son, purifies us from all sin."

Walking in the light is a powerful metaphor for living in the truth and holiness of God. It contrasts the darkness of sin and deception with the clarity and purity of living according to God's ways. This chapter explores what it means to walk in the light, how it impacts our relationships with others, and the continual purification we receive through Jesus Christ.

The Call to Walk in the Light

Walking in the light is an invitation to live in alignment with God's truth and holiness. It involves turning away from the darkness of sin and embracing a life that reflects the character of Christ.

1. Living in Truth: Walking in the light means living in truth. It involves being honest with ourselves, with God, and with others. This truthfulness extends to our thoughts, words, and actions, ensuring that they align with God's Word (John 8:31-32).

2. Pursuing Holiness: To walk in the light is to pursue holiness. It means setting ourselves apart from sinful behaviors and striving to live a life that pleases God. This pursuit requires daily decisions to reject temptation and to follow Christ's example (1 Peter 1:15-16).

3. Reflecting Christ: Walking in the light means reflecting the character of Christ. As we grow in our relationship with Him, His light shines through us, impacting those around us. Our lives should be a testimony of His love, grace, and truth (Matthew 5:14-16).

Fellowship with One Another

Walking in the light not only affects our relationship with God but also our relationships with others. It fosters genuine fellowship and community among believers.

1. Authentic Relationships: When we walk in the light, we cultivate authentic relationships. This involves being open and honest with one another, sharing our struggles, and supporting each other in our spiritual journeys. Authentic relationships are built on trust and transparency (James 5:16).

2. Unity in the Body: Walking in the light promotes unity within the body of Christ. As we align ourselves with God's truth and love, we are united in purpose and mission. This unity is a powerful witness to the world, demonstrating the reality of God's love (Ephesians 4:3).

3. Mutual Encouragement: Fellowship in the light involves mutual encouragement. We are called to build each other up, to spur one another on toward love and good deeds, and to bear each other's burdens. This encouragement strengthens our faith and helps us to persevere (Hebrews 10:24-25).

Continual Purification

One of the most profound aspects of walking in the light is the continual purification we receive through Jesus Christ. His sacrifice on the cross cleanses us from all sin and enables us to live in His light.

1. The Power of Christ's Blood: The blood of Jesus purifies us from all sin. This purification is not a one-time event but a continuous process. As we confess our sins and turn to Him, He faithfully cleanses us and restores our fellowship with God (1 John 1:9).

2. Living in Forgiveness: Walking in the light means living in the forgiveness that Christ offers. We are no longer bound by guilt and shame but are set free to live in His grace.

This freedom allows us to approach God with confidence and to extend forgiveness to others (Ephesians 1:7).

3. Growing in Sanctification: Walking in the light involves growing in sanctification. The Holy Spirit works in us to make us more like Christ, transforming our hearts and minds. This growth in holiness is a lifelong journey that requires our cooperation and dependence on God's power (2 Corinthians 3:18).

Practical Steps to Walk in the Light

To walk in the light, we must take practical steps that align our lives with God's truth and holiness.

1. Daily Devotion: Spending time daily in God's Word and prayer is essential for walking in the light. This devotion strengthens our relationship with Him and equips us to live according to His will. Regular reflection on Scripture helps us to discern truth and to apply it to our lives (Psalm 119:105).

2. Accountability: Accountability is crucial for walking in the light. We need others to hold us accountable, to encourage us, and to challenge us when we stray. Building relationships with fellow believers who will support us in our walk is vital (Proverbs 27:17).

3. Obedience to God's Commands: Walking in the light involves obeying God's commands. This obedience is a response to His love and a demonstration of our commitment

to Him. As we obey His Word, we experience the blessings of living in His light (John 14:15).

4. Confession and Repentance: Regular confession and repentance are necessary for walking in the light. When we fall short, we must turn to God, confess our sins, and seek His forgiveness. This ongoing process keeps our hearts pure and our relationship with God strong (1 John 1:9).

The Impact of Walking in the Light

Walking in the light has a profound impact on our lives and the lives of those around us. It transforms our character, deepens our relationships, and enhances our witness to the world.

1. Transformed Character: As we walk in the light, our character is transformed to reflect Christ. We develop qualities such as love, joy, peace, patience, kindness, goodness, faithfulness, gentleness, and self-control. These qualities testify to the work of the Holy Spirit in our lives (Galatians 5:22-23).

2. Deepened Relationships: Walking in the light deepens our relationships with others. Authentic fellowship, mutual encouragement, and unity strengthen the bonds between believers. These relationships provide support and accountability, helping us to grow in our faith (Hebrews 10:24-25).

3. Enhanced Witness: Our witness to the world is enhanced when we walk in the light. People see the difference that Christ makes in our lives, and they are drawn to His light. Our lives become a testimony of God's love and grace, pointing others to Him (Matthew 5:16).

Walking in the light is a call to live in alignment with God's truth and holiness. It involves living in truth, pursuing holiness, and reflecting Christ in all we do. Walking in the light fosters genuine fellowship with others, promotes unity in the body of Christ, and encourages mutual support. Through the continual purification we receive from Jesus, we are empowered to live in His light. By taking practical steps such as daily devotion, accountability, obedience, and repentance, we can walk in the light and experience its transformative impact. As we walk in the light, our character is transformed, our relationships are deepened, and our witness to the world is enhanced. May we commit to walking in the light, allowing God's truth and holiness to guide our lives and draw others to Him.

CHAPTER 12

MOSES AS GOD'S REPRESENTATIVE

Exodus 7:1: "Then the LORD said to Moses, 'See, I have made you like God to Pharaoh, and your brother Aaron will be your prophet.'"

In this chapter, we will explore the profound statement made by God to Moses, declaring that Moses would be like God to Pharaoh. This statement holds significant implications for understanding the nature of divine representation, authority, and the role of God's chosen leaders. We will delve into why God made this declaration what it reveals about Moses' mission, his relationship with God, and the broader implications for how God works through human agents.

The Context of God's Statement

The context of God's statement to Moses is crucial for understanding its meaning. Moses was called by God to lead the Israelites out of Egypt, where they had been enslaved for centuries. This task required confronting Pharaoh, the powerful ruler of Egypt, and demanding the release of God's people.

1. God's Commission: God called Moses to a unique and challenging mission. From the burning bush encounter to the moment of confrontation with Pharaoh, God equipped Moses with the authority and power needed to accomplish this task (Exodus 3:10).

2. Pharaoh's Resistance: Pharaoh's heart was hardened, and he repeatedly refused to let the Israelites go. This obstinacy set the stage for a series of dramatic confrontations between Moses and Pharaoh, during which God's power and authority would be demonstrated (Exodus 7:13).

Moses as God's Representative

When God said to Moses, "I have made you like God to Pharaoh," He was appointing Moses as His representative. This designation involved several key aspects:

1. Divine Authority: Moses was given divine authority to act on God's behalf. This authority was necessary to confront Pharaoh and to perform the miraculous signs that would demonstrate God's power. Moses' words and actions carried the weight of divine command (Exodus 4:15-16).

2. Mediation Role: Moses served as a mediator between God and both Pharaoh and the Israelites. He communicated God's messages, relayed His commands, and acted as an intermediary in the unfolding events. This role was crucial for ensuring that God's will was clearly conveyed and executed (Exodus 19:3-6).

3. Performing Miracles: God empowered Moses to perform miracles as signs of His divine presence and authority. These miracles, such as turning the Nile into blood and calling down plagues, were meant to compel Pharaoh to acknowledge God's supremacy (Exodus 7:17).

The Significance of Being "Like God"

Being made "like God" to Pharaoh held profound significance for Moses' mission and for understanding how God operates through chosen leaders.

1. Divine Presence: Moses embodied the presence of God in his interactions with Pharaoh. When Pharaoh saw and heard Moses, he was encountering the authority and power of God. This representation was necessary to challenge Pharaoh's belief in his own divinity and to demonstrate the true God's supremacy (Exodus 8:19).

2. God's Spokesperson: As God's spokesperson, Moses' words carried divine authority. He spoke not on his own behalf but as the mouthpiece of God. This role required

Moses to faithfully communicate God's messages without alteration, ensuring that God's will was clearly and accurately conveyed (Exodus 4:12).

3. Illustration of Divine Authority: By making Moses "like God" to Pharaoh, God illustrated the concept of divine authority being delegated to human agents. This delegation is seen throughout the Bible, where prophets, judges, and apostles are empowered to act on God's behalf, carrying His authority and mandate (Jeremiah 1:9-10).

The Broader Implications

God's declaration to Moses has broader implications for understanding how He works through human representatives and the nature of divine authority.

1. Human Agents in God's Plan: Throughout history, God has chosen individuals to carry out His plans and purposes. These human agents, like Moses, are empowered and equipped by God to fulfill their divine missions. Their authority and effectiveness stem from their relationship with God and their obedience to His will (Judges 6:14).

2. Role of Faithfulness: The effectiveness of God's representatives depends on their faithfulness to His commands. Moses' success was tied to his willingness to obey God and to faithfully carry out His instructions. This principle

applies to all who are called to serve God—faithfulness is key to fulfilling one's divine mission (1 Samuel 15:22).

3. God's Authority Delegated: The concept of God delegating His authority to human agents is seen in the New Testament as well. Jesus delegated authority to His disciples, empowering them to preach, heal, and cast out demons in His name. This delegation continues in the church today, where believers are called to act as Christ's ambassadors (Matthew 10:1, 2 Corinthians 5:20).

Moses' Unique Relationship with God

Moses' unique relationship with God is highlighted in this declaration. He was not only a servant but also a friend of God, entrusted with a special mission.

1. Intimacy with God: Moses enjoyed a unique intimacy with God. He spoke with God "face to face, as one speaks to a friend" (Exodus 33:11). This close relationship was the foundation of his authority and effectiveness as God's representative.

2. Trust and Obedience: Moses' trust in God and his obedience to His commands were crucial for his role. Despite his initial reluctance and feelings of inadequacy, Moses ultimately submitted to God's will, demonstrating his faith and reliance on God's power (Exodus 4:10-12).

3. Intercessor for the People: Moses also served as an intercessor for the Israelites. He pleaded with God on their behalf, seeking mercy and forgiveness for their sins. This role further illustrates the mediating function that Moses fulfilled, representing both God to the people and the people to God (Exodus 32:11-14).

Lessons for Believers Today

The story of Moses being made "like God" to Pharaoh provides valuable lessons for believers today about divine representation, authority, and faithfulness.

1. Embracing Our Role: As believers, we are called to represent Christ in the world. This calling involves embodying His love, truth, and authority in our interactions with others. We are to be His ambassadors, carrying His message of reconciliation and salvation (2 Corinthians 5:20).

2. Dependence on God: Like Moses, we must recognize that our effectiveness in representing God depends on our relationship with Him. Intimacy with God through prayer, study of His Word, and obedience to His commands is essential for fulfilling our mission (John 15:5).

3. Faithfulness in Obedience: Faithfulness in obedience is key to being effective representatives of God. We must be committed to following God's instructions and living according to His will. Our faithfulness impacts our

ability to carry out His purposes and to demonstrate His power and love to the world (Luke 16:10).

4. Empowered by the Holy Spirit: Just as Moses was empowered by God to perform miracles and speak with authority, we are empowered by the Holy Spirit. The Holy Spirit equips us with spiritual gifts, guides us in truth, and empowers us to live out our faith boldly (Acts 1:8).

God's declaration to Moses that he would be "like God" to Pharaoh is a profound statement of divine representation and authority. It underscores the importance of obedience, faithfulness, and intimate relationship with God in fulfilling our divine mission. As believers, we are called to represent Christ in the world, empowered by the Holy Spirit and guided by God's Word. By embracing our role, depending on God, and being faithful in our obedience, we can effectively carry out God's purposes and reflect His glory to those around us. May we, like Moses, faithfully serve as God's representatives, bringing His message of love, redemption, and hope to a world in need.

CHAPTER 13

UNDERSTANDING JESUS' STATEMEN, YOU ARE GOD"

John 10:34-35: "Jesus answered them, 'Is it not written in your Law, "I have said you are 'gods'"? If he called them 'gods,' to whom the word of God came—and Scripture cannot be set aside—'"

In John 10:34-35, Jesus makes a profound statement by quoting Psalm 82:6, where it is written, "I have said, you are gods." This statement has led to much discussion and sometimes confusion about its meaning and implications. In this chapter, we will explore the context of Jesus' words, their meaning in the biblical framework, and what they reveal about our identity and responsibility as God's people.

The Context of Jesus' Statement

To understand Jesus' statement, it is essential to look at the context in which He made it. Jesus was responding to the Jewish leaders who accused Him of blasphemy because He claimed to be the Son of God.

1. Accusation of Blasphemy: The Jewish leaders were ready to stone Jesus because they believed He was committing blasphemy by claiming to be one with the Father. They understood His claim as making Himself equal with God (John 10:30-33).

2. Quoting Psalm 82: In His defense, Jesus quoted Psalm 82:6, where God addresses human judges as "gods." By doing this, Jesus highlighted that if human judges could be called "gods" because of their role and authority, it was not blasphemous for Him, the true Son of God, to claim divinity (John 10:34-36).

The Meaning of "You Are Gods" in Psalm 82

Psalm 82 provides the key to understanding Jesus' statement. In this psalm, God stands in the divine assembly and judges the human judges of Israel who were appointed to carry out justice but had failed in their duties.

1. Human Judges as 'Gods': The term "gods" (Elohim) in Psalm 82 refers to human judges or rulers who were given authority to represent God's justice on earth. They were called "gods" because they were entrusted with executing divine judgment and authority (Psalm 82:1-2).

2. Accountability to God: Despite being called "gods," these judges were held accountable by God for their actions. They were expected to defend the weak, uphold justice, and act righteously. Their failure to do so led to God pronouncing judgment on them, reminding them of their mortality (Psalm 82:6-7).

Jesus' Use of Psalm 82

Jesus used Psalm 82 to make a specific point about His identity and mission.

1. Defending His Divinity: By quoting Psalm 82, Jesus argued that if Scripture could refer to human judges as "gods" because of their role, it was not blasphemous for Him, who was sent by the Father and sanctified, to call Himself the Son of God. He emphasized that His works testified to His divine origin and mission (John 10:37-38).

2. Highlighting Misunderstanding: Jesus used the scripture to expose the misunderstanding of the Jewish leaders. They failed to recognize the true nature of His mission and identity, despite the evidence of His works and the fulfillment of prophecy (John 10:25-26).

Implications for Our Identity

Jesus' statement has important implications for our identity as God's people.

1. Role as Representatives: Just as the judges in Psalm 82 were called "gods" because of their role as representatives of God's authority, believers are called to represent God's kingdom on earth. We are entrusted with the mission of reflecting His justice, love, and truth in our lives (2 Corinthians 5:20).

2. Authority and Responsibility: Believers are given authority through Christ to carry out God's will. This includes proclaiming the gospel, exercising spiritual gifts, and living out the principles of God's kingdom. With this authority comes the responsibility to act justly, love mercy, and walk humbly with God (Micah 6:8).

3. Identity in Christ: Our identity is rooted in our relationship with Christ. As children of God, we are called to live in a way that reflects His character and purposes. This identity empowers us to live with confidence, knowing that we are co-heirs with Christ and partakers in His divine nature (Romans 8:17, 2 Peter 1:4).

Walking in Our God-Given Authority

Understanding our God-given authority helps us to live with purpose and impact.

1. Empowered by the Holy Spirit: The Holy Spirit empowers us to fulfill our calling. He equips us with spiritual gifts, guides us into all truth, and strengthens us to overcome

challenges. Walking in the Spirit enables us to exercise our authority effectively (Acts 1:8, Galatians 5:16).

2. Proclaiming the Kingdom: We are called to proclaim the kingdom of God, sharing the good news of Jesus Christ with others. This involves not only preaching but also demonstrating the power and love of God through our actions. Our lives should be a testimony of God's transforming grace (Matthew 28:19-20).

3. Living with Integrity: Exercising our God-given authority requires living with integrity. Our actions should align with our identity in Christ, reflecting His holiness and righteousness. Integrity builds trust and credibility, enhancing our witness to the world (1 Peter 2:12).

The Ultimate Fulfillment in Christ

While human judges in Psalm 82 were called "gods" in a limited sense, Jesus is the ultimate fulfillment of this concept as the true Son of God.

1. Jesus' Unique Divinity: Jesus is not just a representative of God; He is God incarnate. His divinity is unique and unparalleled. He perfectly embodies the character, authority, and power of God. His works, teachings, and resurrection confirm His divine identity (Colossians 2:9).

2. Our Union with Christ: Believers are united with Christ through faith. This union means that we share in His

life, authority, and mission. Our identity is secure in Him, and we are empowered to live out His purposes on earth. This union is both a privilege and a responsibility (Galatians 2:20).

Jesus' statement, "You are gods," as quoted from Psalm 82, highlights the profound responsibility and authority given to God's representatives. While it initially referred to human judges, its ultimate fulfillment is found in Jesus Christ, the true Son of God. As believers, we are called to represent God's kingdom on earth, empowered by the Holy Spirit, and living out our identity in Christ with integrity and purpose. Understanding our God-given authority helps us to walk confidently in our calling, proclaiming the gospel and demonstrating God's love and justice to the world. May we embrace our role as God's representatives, reflecting His character and fulfilling His mission with faithfulness and grace.

CHAPTER 14

THE TRANSFORMING POWER OF GOD'S WORD

Hebrews 4:12: "For the word of God is alive and active. Sharper than any double-edged sword, it penetrates even to dividing soul and spirit, joints and marrow; it judges the thoughts and attitudes of the heart."

God's Word holds transformative power. It is not merely a collection of ancient writings but a living and active force that shapes our lives, molds our character, and directs our paths. In this chapter, we explore the transformative power of God's Word and how it impacts our faith, our minds, and our daily lives.

The Living Nature of God's Word

The Bible describes God's Word as alive and active. This description highlights its dynamic and powerful nature.

1. Alive and Active: The Word of God is not static; it is living and active. It speaks to us today, addressing our

current situations and needs. Its truths are eternal and relevant, capable of bringing life and growth to those who embrace it (Isaiah 55:11).

2. Sharp and Penetrating: God's Word is described as sharper than any double-edged sword. This imagery conveys its ability to penetrate deeply into our hearts and minds, revealing our true thoughts and intentions. It discerns our innermost motives and desires, bringing conviction and transformation (Hebrews 4:12).

3. Judging and Transforming: The Word of God judges the thoughts and attitudes of the heart. It exposes sin, challenges wrong thinking, and guides us toward righteousness. This process of transformation is essential for spiritual growth and maturity (2 Timothy 3:16-17).

The Role of God's Word in Spiritual Growth

Engaging with God's Word is crucial for spiritual growth and transformation. It provides the foundation for our faith and the nourishment for our souls.

1. Foundation of Faith: Faith comes from hearing the message, and the message is heard through the word about Christ (Romans 10:17). God's Word is the foundation upon which our faith is built. It reveals who God is, what He has done, and His promises for us. Through Scripture, we come to know God and trust in His faithfulness.

2. Nourishment for the Soul: Just as physical food sustains our bodies, God's Word nourishes our souls. It provides spiritual sustenance, strength, and encouragement. Regular engagement with Scripture helps us grow in our relationship with God and equips us to face life's challenges (Matthew 4:4).

3. Guide for Living: God's Word serves as a guide for living. It instructs us in righteousness, teaching us how to live in a way that honors God and blesses others. It provides wisdom for decision-making and principles for godly living (Psalm 119:105).

The Power of God's Word in Renewal and Transformation

God's Word has the power to renew our minds and transform our lives. This transformation involves a deep, inner change that aligns us with God's will.

1. Renewing the Mind: Transformation begins with the renewal of our minds. God's Word renews our thinking, replacing lies with truth and aligning our thoughts with His. This renewal leads to a change in our attitudes, perspectives, and behaviors (Romans 12:2).

2. Transforming the Heart: The Word of God transforms our hearts by revealing areas that need change and by planting seeds of righteousness. It shapes our character,

molding us into the likeness of Christ. This transformation is a continual process that requires ongoing engagement with Scripture (Psalm 51:10).

3. Empowering for Action: God's Word not only transforms our inner being but also empowers us for action. It equips us to serve, to witness, and to live out our faith boldly. The transformative power of Scripture compels us to act in accordance with God's will, making a difference in the world (James 1:22-25).

Practical Steps to Engage with God's Word

Engaging with God's Word effectively involves intentional practices that allow its truths to penetrate and transform our lives.

1. Regular Reading: Regular reading of Scripture is foundational. Set aside time each day to read and reflect on God's Word. Consistent reading helps build familiarity with the Bible and allows its truths to permeate your heart and mind (Joshua 1:8).

2. Meditation: Meditation involves pondering and reflecting on Scripture. Take time to think deeply about what you read, considering its implications for your life. Meditation helps internalize God's Word and apply it to daily living (Psalm 1:2).

3. Memorization: Memorizing Scripture is a powerful tool for transformation. It allows you to recall God's Word in times of need, providing guidance, comfort, and strength. Memorization helps embed God's truths deeply within you (Psalm 119:11).

4. Study: Studying the Bible involves a deeper exploration of its meanings and contexts. Use study tools such as commentaries, concordances, and Bible dictionaries to gain a richer understanding of Scripture. Group studies can also provide insights and foster growth (2 Timothy 2:15).

5. Prayer: Prayerfully engage with God's Word. Ask the Holy Spirit to illuminate the Scriptures and to apply its truths to your life. Pray for understanding, wisdom, and the strength to live out what you learn (Ephesians 1:17-18).

The Impact of God's Word on Community

God's Word not only transforms individuals but also impacts the community of believers. It fosters unity, growth, and collective mission.

1. Unity in Truth: God's Word unites believers in truth. As we collectively submit to Scripture, we align ourselves with God's will and purpose. This unity is essential for the health and effectiveness of the church (Ephesians 4:13).

2. Spiritual Growth: Engaging with Scripture as a community fosters spiritual growth. Sharing insights, discussing applications, and encouraging one another in the Word builds up the body of Christ and strengthens our faith (Colossians 3:16).

3. Mission and Witness: The transformative power of God's Word equips the church for its mission. As we live out the truths of Scripture, we become effective witnesses for Christ, demonstrating His love and truth to the world (Matthew 28:19-20).

The transforming power of God's Word is unparalleled. It is alive and active, capable of penetrating our hearts and minds and bringing about profound change. By engaging with Scripture through regular reading, meditation, memorization, study, and prayer, we open ourselves to its transformative work. God's Word renews our minds, transforms our hearts, and empowers us for action, both individually and as a community of believers. May we embrace the power of God's Word, allowing it to shape our lives and to equip us for His purposes. Let us walk in the truth and light of Scripture, experiencing the fullness of life that comes from living according to God's Word.

CHAPTER 15

JUDGING ANGELS

1 Corinthians 6:3: "Do you not know that we will judge angels? How much more the things of this life!"

The Apostle Paul's statement in 1 Corinthians 6:3 is both intriguing and profound. He reminds the Corinthian believers of their future role in judging angels, using this truth to address issues of disputes among believers. This chapter explores the meaning and implications of this statement, our authority in Christ, and how this future role impacts our present lives.

Understanding Paul's Statement

To understand Paul's statement, we need to explore its context and implications.

1. Context of the Statement: Paul made this statement in the context of addressing disputes among believers in the

Corinthian church. Some members were taking their disputes to secular courts rather than resolving them within the church. Paul rebukes them, emphasizing that believers should be capable of judging matters among themselves (1 Corinthians 6:1-2).

2. Future Authority: Paul points to the future authority that believers will have, including the judgment of angels. This reference serves to highlight the dignity and responsibility of believers, suggesting that if they will judge angels in the future, they should be competent to handle earthly disputes now (1 Corinthians 6:4-5).

The Nature of Judging Angels

What does it mean that believers will judge angels? To understand this, we need to consider the broader biblical context.

1. Role in the Final Judgment: The Bible indicates that believers will have a role in the final judgment. This includes judging the world and, as Paul states, judging angels. This suggests that believers will participate with Christ in His ultimate judgment over creation, including the spiritual realm (Matthew 19:28, Revelation 20:4).

2. Judgment of Fallen Angels: The reference to judging angels likely pertains to the judgment of fallen angels—those who rebelled against God along with Satan.

These angels are reserved for judgment, and believers will have a role in this process, affirming God's justice and authority (2 Peter 2:4, Jude 1:6).

3. Authority in Christ: The authority to judge angels stems from our union with Christ. As co-heirs with Christ, believers share in His authority and victory over all spiritual powers. This future role underscores the profound honor and responsibility bestowed upon us as God's children (Romans 8:17, Ephesians 1:20-21).

Implications for Our Present Lives

Understanding our future role in judging angels has significant implications for our present lives and how we live as followers of Christ.

1. Living with Dignity and Responsibility: Knowing that we will judge angels elevates our understanding of our identity and dignity in Christ. It reminds us that we are called to live with integrity, wisdom, and responsibility. Our conduct should reflect our future role and the honor God has bestowed upon us (1 Peter 2:9).

2. Handling Disputes Wisely: Paul uses the truth about judging angels to challenge believers to handle disputes wisely within the church. It emphasizes the importance of resolving conflicts with godly wisdom and justice, rather than relying on secular courts. Believers are called to demonstrate the

principles of God's kingdom in their relationships (1 Corinthians 6:1-5).

3. Exercising Spiritual Authority: Understanding our future role encourages us to exercise spiritual authority in the present. We are called to stand firm against spiritual forces of evil, knowing that we share in Christ's victory. This involves praying with authority, resisting the devil, and living in the power of the Holy Spirit (Ephesians 6:10-18, James 4:7).

4. Preparing for the Future: Our future role in judging angels motivates us to prepare for that responsibility. This preparation involves growing in spiritual maturity, developing godly character, and deepening our understanding of God's Word. As we grow in these areas, we become more equipped to fulfill the roles God has assigned to us (2 Peter 3:18, 2 Timothy 2:15).

The Broader Context of Judgment

To fully grasp the concept of judging angels, we need to understand the broader biblical context of judgment.

1. God's Ultimate Authority: All judgment belongs to God, who is the ultimate Judge of all creation. He exercises perfect justice and righteousness in all His judgments. Our participation in judgment is a delegated authority, granted by God through our union with Christ (Psalm 96:13, John 5:22).

2. Christ's Role in Judgment: Jesus Christ is central to God's judgment. He is the appointed Judge who will execute final judgment on all beings, including angels and humans. Our role in judging angels is a participation in His judgment, reflecting our unity with Him (Acts 17:31, 2 Corinthians 5:10).

3. Purpose of Judgment: The purpose of judgment is to affirm God's justice, to vindicate His holiness, and to establish His kingdom. Judging angels is part of the broader narrative of God's redemptive plan, where all things are brought under Christ's lordship and made right (Revelation 21:1-5).

Living in Light of Our Future Role

As we reflect on our future role in judging angels, we are called to live in a manner worthy of this calling.

1. Pursuing Holiness: Our future role in judgment calls us to pursue holiness in our daily lives. We are to be set apart for God's purposes, living in purity and integrity. Holiness prepares us to exercise our future authority with righteousness (1 Peter 1:15-16).

2. Developing Wisdom: Judging requires wisdom and discernment. We are called to grow in godly wisdom, seeking understanding and knowledge through God's Word and the guidance of the Holy Spirit. This wisdom equips us to handle

present challenges and prepares us for future responsibilities (Proverbs 4:7, James 1:5).

3. Serving with Humility: The authority to judge is not a cause for pride but a call to humble service. Jesus exemplified servant leadership, and we are called to follow His example. Our future role should inspire us to serve others with love, humility, and compassion (Mark 10:42-45, Philippians 2:5-8).

4. Building the Church: Our role in judging angels highlights the importance of building and strengthening the church. We are to edify one another, promote unity, and work together for the advancement of God's kingdom. A strong and healthy church reflects God's glory and prepares us for our future roles (Ephesians 4:11-13).

Paul's statement that believers will judge angels is a profound revelation of our future authority and responsibility in Christ. It underscores the dignity and honor bestowed upon us as God's children and calls us to live with integrity, wisdom, and holiness. Understanding this future role impacts our present lives, motivating us to handle disputes wisely, exercise spiritual authority, and prepare for our divine responsibilities. As we live in light of our future role, may we pursue holiness, develop wisdom, serve with humility, and

build the church, reflecting the character and purposes of our
Lord Jesus Christ.

CHAPTER 16

WE ARE KINGS AND PRIESTS

Revelation 1:6: "And hath made us kings and priests unto God and his Father; to him be glory and dominion for ever and ever. Amen."

The Bible describes believers as both kings and priests, a profound dual identity that carries significant implications for our lives and service to God. This chapter explores the meaning of being kings and priests, the responsibilities and privileges associated with these roles, and how they shape our daily living and spiritual growth.

The Identity of Kings and Priests

The roles of kings and priests in the biblical context provide a rich understanding of our identity in Christ.

1. Kings: As kings, we share in Christ's authority and are called to reign with Him. This royal identity reflects our position in God's kingdom and our role in exercising His

authority on earth. It emphasizes our dignity, responsibility, and the call to lead and serve with integrity (Revelation 5:10).

2. Priests: As priests, we have direct access to God and the privilege of ministering to Him and others. This priestly role involves intercession, offering spiritual sacrifices, and living a life of worship and holiness. It highlights our intimate relationship with God and our role in representing Him to the world (1 Peter 2:9).

The Responsibilities of Kings

Our identity as kings comes with significant responsibilities that align with God's purposes and kingdom values.

1. Exercising Authority: As kings, we are called to exercise authority in alignment with God's will. This involves making decisions, leading others, and influencing our spheres of influence with godly principles. Our authority is derived from our relationship with Christ and must reflect His character and justice (Matthew 28:18-20).

2. Stewardship: Kingship involves stewardship of the resources and opportunities God has entrusted to us. We are to manage our time, talents, finances, and relationships in a way that honors God and advances His kingdom. Faithful stewardship is a mark of our commitment to God's purposes (Matthew 25:14-30).

3. Leadership and Service: As kings, we are called to lead by serving. Jesus exemplified servant leadership, teaching that true greatness is found in serving others. Our leadership should be characterized by humility, compassion, and a desire to uplift and empower those we lead (Mark 10:42-45).

The Responsibilities of Priests

Our identity as priests involves specific responsibilities that deepen our relationship with God and enhance our ministry to others.

1. Intercession: Priests are called to intercede on behalf of others, bringing their needs and concerns before God. This ministry of prayer is a powerful way to support and encourage others, seeking God's intervention and blessing in their lives (1 Timothy 2:1).

2. Spiritual Sacrifices: As priests, we offer spiritual sacrifices to God. These sacrifices include our worship, praise, acts of service, and living a holy life. They are expressions of our devotion and gratitude to God, offered through Jesus Christ (Hebrews 13:15-16).

3. Holiness and Purity: Priests are called to live lives of holiness and purity, set apart for God's purposes. This involves pursuing righteousness, avoiding sin, and striving to reflect God's character in all we do. Holiness is essential for

effective ministry and a closer walk with God (1 Peter 1:15-16).

The Privileges of Kings and Priests

Along with responsibilities, our identity as kings and priests comes with profound privileges that enrich our spiritual lives.

1. Access to God: As priests, we have direct access to God through Jesus Christ. This access allows us to approach God's throne with confidence, receive His grace and mercy, and commune with Him intimately. It is a privilege that transforms our prayer life and worship (Hebrews 4:16).

2. Joint-Heirs with Christ: As kings, we are joint-heirs with Christ, sharing in His inheritance and authority. This privilege assures us of our eternal destiny and the blessings of God's kingdom. It gives us confidence and hope, knowing that we are co-heirs with the King of kings (Romans 8:17).

3. Empowerment by the Holy Spirit: Both our kingly and priestly roles are empowered by the Holy Spirit. The Spirit equips us with spiritual gifts, guides us in truth, and empowers us to live out our calling effectively. His presence is essential for fulfilling our responsibilities and experiencing the fullness of our identity in Christ (Acts 1:8).

Living Out Our Identity

Understanding our identity as kings and priests shapes how we live and serve God daily.

1. Walking in Authority: We are called to walk in the authority given to us by Christ. This involves standing firm in our faith, resisting the enemy, and proclaiming God's truth with boldness. Walking in authority means living with the confidence that comes from knowing our position in Christ (Ephesians 6:10-18).

2. Serving with Compassion: Our leadership and priestly ministry should be marked by compassion. We are to serve others with love, humility, and a genuine desire to meet their needs. Compassionate service reflects the heart of Jesus and draws others to Him (Colossians 3:12-14).

3. Pursuing Holiness: Holiness is foundational to our identity as priests. We are called to live lives that honor God, avoid sin, and strive for righteousness. Pursuing holiness involves daily surrender to God, allowing Him to transform us by His Spirit (Romans 12:1-2).

4. Interceding for Others: As priests, intercession is a vital part of our ministry. We are to pray fervently for others, lifting up their needs and seeking God's intervention. Intercessory prayer is an act of love and a powerful way to support and bless others (James 5:16).

5. Worshiping Wholeheartedly: Our priestly role involves offering wholehearted worship to God. Worship is not just a Sunday activity but a lifestyle of devotion, gratitude, and reverence. It is an expression of our love for God and our response to His goodness and grace (John 4:23-24).

The Impact of Our Identity

Living as kings and priests has a transformative impact on our lives and the world around us.

1. Transformation of Society: As kings, we are called to influence society with godly values and principles. Our leadership and decisions can bring about positive change, reflecting God's justice, mercy, and truth. By living out our identity, we contribute to the transformation of our communities and the world (Micah 6:8).

2. Building the Church: As priests, we play a crucial role in building and edifying the church. Our ministry of intercession, service, and spiritual sacrifices strengthens the body of Christ and fosters spiritual growth. By fulfilling our priestly duties, we help create a vibrant, healthy church community (Ephesians 4:11-13).

3. Witness to the World: Our identity as kings and priests is a powerful witness to the world. When we live out our calling with integrity, compassion, and holiness, we demonstrate the reality of God's kingdom. Our lives become

a testimony of God's love, grace, and transformative power, drawing others to Him (Matthew 5:16).

The identity of believers as kings and priests is a profound and empowering truth. It encompasses both the authority to lead and serve as kings and the privilege to minister and intercede as priests. This dual identity shapes our responsibilities, privileges, and daily living, calling us to walk in authority, serve with compassion, pursue holiness, and worship wholeheartedly. As we embrace our roles as kings and priests, we experience the fullness of our identity in Christ and make a transformative impact on the world around us. May we faithfully live out this calling, bringing glory to God and advancing His kingdom on earth.

CHAPTER 17

THE "GOD'S" AS SUPERNATURAL BEINGS

Psalm 82:1: "God presides in the great assembly; he gives judgment among the gods."

Psalm 82 presents a fascinating picture of a divine assembly where God stands in judgment over other supernatural beings referred to as "gods." This chapter delves into the identity of these "gods," their roles, and the implications of God's judgment upon them. Understanding this passage offers profound insights into the spiritual realm and God's supreme authority over all creation.

The Divine Assembly

Psalm 82:1 introduces the scene of a divine assembly, a council of supernatural beings over which God presides. This concept of a divine council is found in various parts of the Bible and ancient Near Eastern literature.

1. The Concept of the Divine Council: The divine council consists of supernatural beings who serve God and carry out His will. These beings are often referred to as "sons of God" or "gods" and are depicted as participating in God's heavenly court (Job 1:6, Psalm 89:5-7).

2. God's Supreme Authority: God is depicted as the supreme ruler who presides over this assembly. His authority is unmatched, and He exercises judgment over the other members of the council. This scene underscores God's sovereignty and ultimate control over all spiritual beings (Psalm 82:1).

Identity of the "Gods"

The term "gods" (Elohim) in Psalm 82:1 refers to these supernatural beings. Understanding their identity and role in the biblical narrative helps to clarify their significance.

1. Supernatural Beings: The "gods" in Psalm 82 are supernatural beings created by God. They are distinct from human beings and possess significant power and authority in the spiritual realm. These beings are part of the heavenly host that serves and worships God (Psalm 103:20-21).

2. Rulers and Authorities: These supernatural beings are often associated with ruling and governing various aspects of creation under God's authority. They are sometimes depicted as having jurisdiction over nations or regions,

executing divine decrees, and maintaining order in the spiritual and earthly realms (Daniel 10:13, 20-21).

3. Fallen and Rebellious Beings: Some of these supernatural beings rebelled against God and became adversaries to His purposes. These fallen beings, often referred to as demons or principalities, seek to thwart God's plans and deceive humanity (Ephesians 6:12, Jude 1:6).

God's Judgment Among the "Gods"

Psalm 82:1 emphasizes God's role as the judge of these supernatural beings. This judgment is based on their failure to fulfill their God-given responsibilities.

1. Failure to Execute Justice: In Psalm 82, God rebukes these "gods" for failing to uphold justice and protect the weak and vulnerable. They are accused of partiality, corruption, and neglecting their duties. God's judgment is a response to their failure to reflect His character and execute His justice (Psalm 82:2-4).

2. Pronouncement of Judgment: God pronounces judgment upon these beings, declaring that despite their exalted status, they will fall and perish like mortal men. This judgment underscores the accountability of all beings, regardless of their power, to God's righteous standards (Psalm 82:6-7).

3. Vindication of God's Justice: God's judgment serves to vindicate His justice and reassert His supreme authority. It demonstrates that all creation, including supernatural beings, is subject to His righteous rule and that He will not tolerate injustice or rebellion (Psalm 82:8).

The Implications for Believers

Understanding the concept of the "gods" and God's judgment upon them has several implications for believers today.

1. Recognizing Spiritual Realities: Believers must recognize the reality of the spiritual realm and the existence of supernatural beings. This awareness helps to understand the spiritual battles that occur and the need for vigilance and reliance on God's power (Ephesians 6:10-18).

2. Trusting in God's Sovereignty: The depiction of God presiding over the divine council reinforces His sovereignty over all creation. Believers can trust that God is in control, even over the spiritual forces that oppose His will. His ultimate victory is assured (Colossians 2:15).

3. Upholding Justice: Just as God expects the "gods" to execute justice, He calls believers to act justly and defend the oppressed. We are to reflect God's character in our actions, standing against injustice and corruption in all forms (Micah 6:8).

4. Accountability to God: The judgment of the "gods" serves as a reminder that all beings are accountable to God. Believers must live with an awareness of this accountability, striving to fulfill their God-given responsibilities and walk in obedience to His commands (2 Corinthians 5:10).

The Broader Biblical Context

The theme of divine councils and the role of supernatural beings is echoed throughout the Bible, providing a broader context for understanding Psalm 82.

1. Job and the Sons of God: In the book of Job, the "sons of God" present themselves before the Lord, and Satan is among them. This scene illustrates the heavenly court and God's interaction with these beings, highlighting their role and God's supreme authority (Job 1:6-12).

2. Daniel and the Princes: In the book of Daniel, the prophet describes spiritual battles involving angelic beings and the "princes" of Persia and Greece. These passages reveal the influence of supernatural beings over earthly affairs and God's intervention through His messengers (Daniel 10:13, 20-21).

3. Revelation and the Heavenly Court: The book of Revelation provides vivid imagery of the heavenly court, with beings such as the 24 elders and the four living creatures worshiping God. These scenes underscore the majesty of

God's throne and the role of supernatural beings in His divine plan (Revelation 4:1-11).

Living in Light of Spiritual Realities

As believers, understanding the spiritual realm and the role of supernatural beings informs how we live our faith and engage in spiritual warfare.

1. Spiritual Discernment: We are called to develop spiritual discernment, recognizing the influence of both godly and ungodly supernatural forces. This discernment helps us navigate spiritual battles and remain steadfast in our faith (1 John 4:1).

2. Prayer and Intercession: Prayer is a powerful tool in engaging the spiritual realm. Through prayer, we seek God's intervention, protection, and guidance. Intercessory prayer also plays a vital role in standing against the spiritual forces of darkness and seeking God's justice (Ephesians 6:18).

3. Spiritual Armor: Believers are instructed to put on the full armor of God to stand firm against spiritual attacks. This armor includes truth, righteousness, the gospel of peace, faith, salvation, the Word of God, and prayer. Equipping ourselves with these spiritual resources is essential for victory in spiritual warfare (Ephesians 6:13-17).

Psalm 82 offers a compelling glimpse into the spiritual realm, where God presides over a divine assembly and judges the "gods." These supernatural beings, entrusted with significant authority, are held accountable to God's righteous standards. For believers, this passage underscores the reality of the spiritual realm, the sovereignty of God, and the call to live justly and faithfully. As we recognize our role in God's kingdom and engage in spiritual warfare, we can trust in His ultimate authority and victory. May we live with spiritual discernment, uphold justice, and rely on God's power as we navigate the complexities of the spiritual and earthly realms.

CHAPTER 18

YAHWEH, THE ELOHIM ABOVE ALL ELOHIM

Psalm 95:3: "For the LORD is the great God, the great King above all gods."

The term "Elohim" is used in the Bible to refer to God, as well as to other spiritual beings such as angels. This chapter explores the meaning and usage of the term "Elohim," highlighting Yahweh's supreme authority as the Elohim above all Elohim. We will delve into the significance of this title, its implications for understanding God's nature and supremacy, and the roles of other spiritual beings referred to as Elohim in the Scriptures.

Understanding "Elohim"

The Hebrew word "Elohim" is a plural form that is often used to refer to God (Yahweh) in the singular sense. It can also refer to other divine or spiritual beings, depending on the context.

1. Elohim as God: When referring to Yahweh, "Elohim" denotes the one true God, the Creator and Sustainer of all things. Despite its plural form, it is used with singular verbs and adjectives when referring to the God of Israel, emphasizing His unique and singular nature (Genesis 1:1).

2. Elohim as Spiritual Beings: The term "Elohim" is also used to describe other spiritual beings, such as angels, judges, and even the spirits of the dead. In these contexts, it highlights their divine or supernatural nature but clearly distinguishes them from Yahweh, who is supreme over all (Psalm 82:1, Job 1:6).

Yahweh, the Supreme Elohim

Psalm 95:3 proclaims Yahweh as the "great God, the great King above all gods." This declaration emphasizes His supremacy over all other spiritual beings referred to as Elohim.

1. Supremacy Over All: Yahweh's supremacy is a central theme in Scripture. He is the Creator of all things, including the spiritual realm and its inhabitants. His authority and power are unmatched, and He alone is worthy of worship and adoration (Isaiah 45:5-7).

2. The Great King: As the great King, Yahweh rules over all creation with justice and righteousness. His

sovereignty extends over the heavens and the earth, and He exercises His dominion with perfect wisdom and love (Psalm 47:2, Daniel 4:34-35).

3. Uniqueness of Yahweh: While there are other Elohim, Yahweh is unique and incomparable. He alone is self-existent, eternal, and unchanging. The Bible emphasizes that there is no other god like Yahweh, who alone is the true and living God (Deuteronomy 6:4, Isaiah 40:25-26).

The Roles of Other Elohim

The term "Elohim" is also used to describe various spiritual beings who serve different roles in the divine order.

1. Angels: In the book of Job, the term "Elohim" is used to refer to angels, also called "sons of God." These heavenly beings serve as messengers and servants of Yahweh, executing His will and assisting His people (Job 1:6, 38:7).

2. Heavenly Assembly: Psalm 82 describes a divine council where God stands in judgment among the elohim. These beings, likely angelic or divine representatives, are called to uphold justice and righteousness. Their failure to do so results in God's rebuke and judgment (Psalm 82:1-7).

3. Other Divine Beings: In some contexts, elohim can refer to other divine beings or spirits, such as those of deceased humans or pagan gods. These beings are

acknowledged but are clearly subordinate to Yahweh and subject to His authority (1 Samuel 28:13, Exodus 12:12).

Implications for Believers

Understanding Yahweh as the supreme Elohim above all Elohim has profound implications for our faith and worship.

1. Exclusive Worship: Recognizing Yahweh's supremacy calls for exclusive worship. Believers are to worship and serve Yahweh alone, rejecting all forms of idolatry and acknowledging Him as the one true God (Exodus 20:3-5, Matthew 4:10).

2. Trust in God's Sovereignty: Knowing that Yahweh is the supreme Elohim assures us of His control over all circumstances. We can trust in His sovereignty, knowing that He governs all things with wisdom and purpose and that nothing can thwart His plans (Romans 8:28, Psalm 135:5-6).

3. Confidence in Spiritual Warfare: Understanding the hierarchy of the spiritual realm gives us confidence in spiritual warfare. While there are other spiritual beings, Yahweh's authority is supreme, and believers are equipped with His power to stand against the forces of darkness (Ephesians 6:10-18, Colossians 2:15).

4. Living in Holiness: Recognizing Yahweh's holiness and supremacy calls us to live in holiness and obedience. As

His people, we are called to reflect His character, uphold His commandments, and live in a manner that honors Him (1 Peter 1:15-16, Micah 6:8).

The Broader Biblical Context

The supremacy of Yahweh as the Elohim above all elohim is a consistent theme throughout the Bible, reflecting His ultimate authority and unique nature.

1. Yahweh's Sovereignty in Creation: The creation narrative establishes Yahweh's sovereignty over all things. He speaks creation into existence, demonstrating His unmatched power and authority over the physical and spiritual realms (Genesis 1:1-31, John 1:1-3).

2. Yahweh's Supremacy in History: Throughout biblical history, Yahweh's supremacy is displayed in His acts of deliverance, judgment, and covenant faithfulness. From the Exodus to the resurrection of Jesus, God's actions reveal His sovereign rule and commitment to His people (Exodus 14:30-31, Acts 2:32-36).

3. Yahweh's Ultimate Victory: The prophetic and apocalyptic literature of the Bible points to Yahweh's ultimate victory over all evil and the establishment of His eternal kingdom. These writings assure believers of God's final triumph and the restoration of all things under His rule (Revelation 21:1-7, Daniel 7:13-14).

Worshiping Yahweh, the Supreme Elohim

Our response to Yahweh's supremacy should be one of awe, worship, and devotion.

1. Reverence and Awe: Recognizing Yahweh's greatness and holiness should lead us to approach Him with reverence and awe. Our worship should reflect His majesty and our deep respect for His divine nature (Hebrews 12:28-29, Psalm 96:9).

2. Wholehearted Worship: Worshiping Yahweh involves our whole being—heart, soul, mind, and strength. We are called to love Him with all that we are, offering our lives as living sacrifices in response to His goodness and sovereignty (Mark 12:30, Romans 12:1-2).

3. Faithful Service: Worshiping Yahweh also means serving Him faithfully. We are to live out our faith through acts of service, justice, and love, reflecting His character in our interactions with others (James 1:27, Matthew 25:34-40).

Yahweh, the Elohim above all elohim, stands supreme over all creation, both visible and invisible. Understanding His unique and unparalleled authority deepens our worship, strengthens our faith, and guides our daily lives. As we recognize His sovereignty and supreme power, we are called to exclusive worship, trust in His control, confidence in spiritual warfare, and a commitment to live in holiness. Let us worship Yahweh with reverence and awe, acknowledging Him as the great King above all gods, and live our lives in faithful service to His glorious name.

CONCLUSION

LIVING AS GOD'S BELOVED

1 Corinthians 6:19-20: "Do you not know that your bodies are temples of the Holy Spirit, who is in you, whom you have received from God? You are not your own; you were bought at a price. Therefore honor God with your bodies."

Understanding that we are God's beloved children fundamentally transforms how we live. This profound truth compels us to honor God in every aspect of our lives, knowing that we belong to Him. Our identity as God's beloved provides security, purpose, and hope, equipping us to be powerful witnesses of His love and grace to a world in need.

Our Identity as God's Beloved

The foundation of our identity is rooted in being God's beloved children. This identity shapes our understanding of who we are and how we live.

1. Temples of the Holy Spirit: As believers, our bodies are temples of the Holy Spirit. This means that God Himself dwells within us, sanctifying us and empowering us to live according to His will. Our lives should reflect the holiness and purity that befits a temple of the living God (1 Corinthians 3:16-17).

2. Bought at a Price: We were bought at a price—the precious blood of Jesus Christ. This sacrificial act underscores our value to God and the depth of His love for us. Recognizing this, we should live in a manner that honors the sacrifice made for our redemption (1 Peter 1:18-19).

3. Not Our Own: Understanding that we are not our own but belong to God changes our perspective on life. We are stewards of the lives, bodies, and resources God has entrusted to us. This stewardship calls for a life of obedience, worship, and service (Romans 14:7-8).

Honoring God with Our Bodies

Our identity as God's beloved compels us to honor Him in all we do, including how we treat our bodies.

1. Purity and Holiness: As temples of the Holy Spirit, we are called to live in purity and holiness. This involves avoiding sinful behaviors and striving to live in a way that reflects God's character. Our conduct should be a testament

to the transformative power of the Holy Spirit within us (1 Thessalonians 4:3-5).

2. Healthy Living: Honoring God with our bodies also includes caring for our physical health. This means making choices that promote physical well-being, such as proper nutrition, exercise, and rest. Our bodies are instruments for God's service, and maintaining their health enables us to serve Him effectively (3 John 1:2).

3. Respect for Others: Honoring God with our bodies involves respecting others. This includes maintaining healthy boundaries, treating others with dignity and respect, and using our bodies to serve and bless others. Our interactions should reflect the love and grace of Christ (1 Corinthians 6:18, 1 Peter 3:8-9).

Living with Purpose and Hope

Embracing our identity as God's beloved gives us a sense of purpose and hope that transforms how we approach life.

1. Purposeful Living: Knowing that we belong to God gives our lives purpose. We are called to live for His glory, using our gifts, talents, and resources to advance His kingdom. This purpose drives us to make choices that align with His will and to seek opportunities to serve Him and others (Ephesians 2:10).

2. Hope in Christ: Our identity as God's beloved provides a secure hope that transcends earthly circumstances. This hope is anchored in the promises of God and the assurance of eternal life with Him. It gives us strength to endure trials, confidence in the face of uncertainty, and joy in all circumstances (Hebrews 6:19-20).

3. Witness to the World: Living as God's beloved makes us powerful witnesses of His love and grace. Our lives should reflect the transformation that comes from knowing Christ, and drawing others to Him. By living out our identity authentically, we testify to the reality of God's love and the hope found in Him (Matthew 5:14-16).

Practical Steps to Live as God's Beloved

Living as God's beloved involves practical steps that help us honor Him and reflect our identity in Christ.

1. Daily Devotion: Spend time daily in God's Word and prayer. This devotion strengthens our relationship with Him, renews our minds, and equips us to live according to His will. Regular communion with God helps us stay grounded in our identity and purpose (Psalm 119:105).

2. Community Engagement: Engage with a community of believers who can support, encourage, and hold you accountable. Fellowship with other Christians

provides a network of support and opportunities to grow together in faith (Hebrews 10:24-25).

3. Service and Outreach: Look for ways to serve others and share the love of Christ. Whether through church ministries, community service, or personal acts of kindness, serving others is a practical expression of our faith and identity as God's beloved (Galatians 5:13).

4. Holistic Care: Take care of your body, mind, and spirit. Practice healthy living, engage in activities that promote mental and emotional well-being, and cultivate spiritual disciplines that draw you closer to God. Holistic care honors God and enables you to live fully for Him (1 Thessalonians 5:23).

5. Obedience to God's Commands: Live in obedience to God's Word. His commands are given for our good and His glory. Obeying His Word demonstrates our love for Him and our commitment to live as His beloved children (John 14:15).

The Transformative Impact

Living as God's beloved has a transformative impact on our lives and the world around us.

1. Personal Transformation: Embracing our identity as God's beloved transforms our character, attitudes, and behaviors. We become more like Christ, exhibiting the fruit

of the Spirit and reflecting His love in all we do (Galatians 5:22-23).

2. Relational Transformation: Our relationships are transformed as we live out our identity in Christ. We learn to love, forgive, and serve others with the same grace we have received. Our interactions become opportunities to reflect God's love and build meaningful connections (Ephesians 4:31-32).

3. Cultural Transformation: As we live as God's beloved, we contribute to the transformation of culture. Our commitment to justice, compassion, and righteousness influences the world around us, bringing light to darkness and hope to the hopeless (Micah 6:8).

Living as God's beloved is a profound and transformative calling. It compels us to honor God in all we do, knowing that we belong to Him and have been bought at a price. Our identity as God's beloved children provides security, purpose, and hope, equipping us to be powerful witnesses of His love and grace to a world in need. As we embrace this truth and live it out daily, we experience personal transformation, build meaningful relationships, and contribute to the cultural change that reflects God's kingdom. May we fully embrace our identity as God's beloved, living lives that honor Him and draw others to the saving knowledge of Jesus Christ.

ADDITIONAL RESOURCES

Recommended Readings for Further Study

1. "Knowing God" by J.I. Packer

- This classic work explores the nature and character of God, helping believers deepen their understanding and relationship with Him.

2. "The Knowledge of the Holy" by A.W. Tozer

- Tozer's insightful book delves into the attributes of God, encouraging a deeper reverence and awe for the divine.

3. "Mere Christianity" by C.S. Lewis

- A foundational apologetic work that explains the basics of Christian belief and the nature of God.

4. "Systematic Theology" by Wayne Grudem

- A comprehensive and accessible guide to Christian theology, covering a wide range of topics including the nature of God, salvation, and the end times.

5. "The Holiness of God" by R.C. Sproul

- This book explores the concept of God's holiness and its implications for believers.

6. "Desiring God" by John Piper

- Piper's work focuses on finding joy in God and living a life that glorifies Him.

7. "The Divine Conspiracy" by Dallas Willard

- Willard's book offers a profound look at the teachings of Jesus and how they apply to modern Christian living.

8. "Experiencing God" by Henry Blackaby and Claude King

- A practical guide to knowing and doing the will of God, emphasizing a personal relationship with Him.

Glossary of Theological Terms

- Atonement: The reconciliation between God and humanity brought about by the sacrificial death of Jesus Christ.

- Canon: The collection of books that are accepted as the inspired and authoritative Word of God.

- Christology: The study of the person and work of Jesus Christ.

- Doctrine: A set of beliefs held and taught by a church, denomination, or religious group.

- Eschatology: The study of the end times, including the return of Christ and the final judgment.

- Exegesis: The critical interpretation and explanation of a biblical text.

- Grace: The unmerited favor of God towards humanity, often associated with salvation.

- Incarnation: The doctrine that the Son of God became human in the person of Jesus Christ.

- Justification: The act by which God declares a sinner righteous based on faith in Jesus Christ.

- Sanctification: The process of being made holy, involving the believer's growth in godliness and obedience to God.

- Theology: The study of the nature of God and religious belief.

- Trinity: The Christian doctrine that God exists as three persons—Father, Son, and Holy Spirit—but is one God.

- Redemption: The action of saving or being saved from sin, error, or evil, often specifically referring to Christ's sacrifice.

- Soteriology: The study of salvation, especially as achieved through Jesus Christ.

- Eucharist: Also known as Communion or the Lord's Supper, it is a Christian sacrament commemorating the Last Supper of Jesus Christ with His disciples.

- Propitiation: The action of appeasing a god, spirit, or person; in Christianity, it specifically refers to the appeasement of God's wrath through the sacrifice of Jesus.

- Revelation: The disclosure of divine truth, often referring to the Bible as God's revealed Word.

- Immutability: The attribute of God that denotes He is unchanging in His nature, character, and purposes.

This appendix provides resources and definitions to aid further study and understanding of the theological concepts discussed in this book. By delving deeper into these topics and familiarizing yourself with key terms, you can enhance your knowledge and strengthen your faith. Use these resources as a foundation for your ongoing spiritual journey, and may they help you grow closer to God and live out your identity as His beloved.